DYNAMO DIARIES

DYNAMO DIARIES

V2

Success Secrets
of 21 Shining Stars!

Compiled & Introduction by:
James Erdt

Copyright ©2017 DYNAMO Publishing
All rights reserved.

Compiled & Introduction by: James Erdt

Printed by Printing Icon.
Available from Amazon.com / Amazon.ca

This book may not be reproduced in whole or in part, in any form or by any means, electronic or mechanical, including photocopying, recording or by any infomation storage and retrieval system now known or hereafter invented, without written permission from the publisher.

DYNAMO Publishing & Creatives CEO is James Erdt.
Cover design and layout by DYNAMO Creatives.
Editor-in-Chief: Nicola Brasil
All photographs are copyright of the co-authors.
DYNAMO Publishing & DYNAMO Creatives are divisions of
DYNAMO Entrepreneur *(DYNAMOentrepreneur.com)*

ISBN-13: 978-1543258646
ISBN-10: 1543258646

WELCOME to the *DYNAMO Diaries*! This project is specifically designed to inspire you to BE THE BEST VERSION OF YOU by learning through the success of others.

I am your host, James Erdt, the Chief Architect of WOW for DYNAMO Entrepreneur, a company that focuses on social entrepreneurs who are "Living Well & Doing Good" around the world. Team DYNAMO is absolutely thrilled to share the second group of 21 uber-talented co-authors in DYNAMO Diaries Volume 2 with you. This compilation is part of an epic series of seven books showcasing nuggets of wisdom that have made each writer successful throughout their life's journey.

A true DYNAMO Entrepreneur's vision of health, wealth and life-balance in this modern information age should be about EVEN MORE free time and EVEN MORE mobility to enjoy mini-retirements and extended vacations, while living life to the fullest versus saving all the gold necessary for the illusion of a safe retirement later in life, with a very unpredictable and unsecured future.

Life is meant to be lived NOW. By investing in things such as your body, mind, spirit and well-being PLUS precious memories with family/friends and relationship capital, you will be much happier, more fulfilled and authentically abundant. True success is an ongoing journey; it is not a destination far away in the unwritten future. Lasting happiness is a choice. Your choice. Here and now.

This book will act as an oxygen mask; it will revive you and inspire you to live a healthy, active life of walking the talk so you can feel alive—and thrive. Regardless of the decisions you made or what happened to you in the past, you can turn your life around in light speed simply by making a choice to do so. Start today. Get over your own negativity; stop playing the blame game, the victim role and that horrible disease known as *"excusitist."* The only person you truly have control over is yourself. Be the change!

This book will support you to take charge of those passion projects you've always wanted to do. It will help you to correct your course along the way instead of never ever getting started and living a life of regret. You can create your dream vision board of achievement and truly see what it feels like to be, to do and have the life you've always dreamed of.

Focus on good and smart balanced choices in the moment, making one proper decision after the next with positive reinforcement and affirmative action, in order to live life with confidence as you move towards your goals. Get ready to get uncomfortable and push past the limits you have imposed upon yourself. That's how you grow. That's how you evolve. That's how you thrive!

The DYNAMO Diaries co-authors will share tips, tricks and their success secrets so you too can positively experience the best life has to offer. They'll teach you about self-reliance, as we all need to remember that it's not about the resources you have, it's about how resourceful you are. These authors support your understanding regarding results and effectiveness. They will help you to work smarter versus working harder and sometimes moving in the wrong direction. They will guide you to live in abundance versus scarcity. Each author thoroughly enjoys supporting others, bringing them great satisfaction and fulfillment knowing that they are giving back to others—which is what life is all about.

We are the DYNAMO Tribe and our DYNAMO Diaries are dedicated to you, our valued reader. Enjoy!

Discover / Develop / Deliver,

James Erdt

Chief Architect of WOW

DYNAMO Entrepreneur

NOTE: *To discover and learn more about the multiple DYNAMO Divisions that support business professionals and small business owners across the board with leading edge products, exceptional services and empowering events, please visit DYNAMOentrepreneur.com and sign up for the mailing list to stay up to speed with everything DYNAMO. Also see and contribute online to #DYNAMOtribe.*

Table of Contents

~

Simple Tips To Find You More Money 13
By Aaron Chan

Cardamon 21
By Aditya Aman

Your Soul Has A Plan For You 29
By Anna DeSantis

I've Been On A Mission 37
By Anne Gagnon

The Secret Is To Give And Receive 45
By Dr. Elio Franco Filice

5 Steps To Achieving Anything You Want! 53
By Frank D'Urzo

It Hasn't Always Been This Way 61
By Joel Martin

Humble Beginnings 69
By Dr. Joseph Radice

Come Out, Come Out, Wherever You Are! 75
By Karen Kessler

Quantum Leadership™ 85
By Dr. Kim Redman

If Today Was My Last Day 95
By Kirillos Shahata

Proven Secrets To Success 101
By Laura Arci

Kick Back 111
By Lize DelaRey Barkhuysen

Excerpt from 'Memoirs of Michelle' 119
By Michelle Biggers

The Hero Within 127
By Parmida Barez

Our True Purpose 135
By Pat Di Rauso

Harnessing Your Inner Leader 145
By Rick Denley

Becoming The Reawakened Spirit Warrior 155
By Rita Aldo Rasi

The Eagle In You 165
By Steven Kerr

Dedication To Success Is A Choice 173
By Tracey McLeod

Wisdom From Within 181
By Zak Lioutas

DYNAMO
DIARIES

V2

Success Secrets
of 21 Shining Stars!

Dedicated to the social entrepreneurs around the globe who are truly making a positive difference by
"Living Well & Doing Good!"

Simple Tips To Find You More Money

~

By Aaron Chan

I've always wanted to go on an epic journey. I've always wanted to save the damsel in distress. I've always wanted to fight against evil. I've always wanted to find the treasure. I've always wanted to solve the mystery. I've always wanted to leap tall buildings. I've always wanted to save the world. I've always wanted to soar. I've always wanted to fly. I've always wanted to explore the ocean. I've always wanted to win in battle. I've always wanted to do great things. I've always wanted to be great. I've always wanted to be proud. I've always wanted to shine in the world. I've always wanted to make a difference. I've always wanted to do something worth dying and living for. I've always wanted to hit a home run. I've always wanted to hoist the cup. I've always wanted to stand on the podium and sing my nation's song. I've always wanted to break-dance. I've always wanted to make beautiful music. I've always wanted to capture stunning images. I've always wanted to make others smile. I've always wanted to make others laugh. I've always wanted to make other love. I've always wanted to climb mountains. I've always wanted to float on a cloud. I've always wanted to make a wish upon a star. I've always wanted to walk on the moon. I've always wanted to go where no-one has gone before. I've always wanted to be a hero. I've always want to do a triple back flip. I've always wanted to see things that others couldn't. I've always wanted to do the impossible. I've always wanted to find that one special person to spend the rest of my life with. I've always wanted to be proud father. I've always wanted to write a book.

Well, you gotta start somewhere...

My name is Aaron Chan. Who knows what people will be calling me tomorrow and who cares what people called me yesterday. Today, people call me "Numbers" and my epic journey includes a sharpened pencil and a finely tuned calculator.

I am a Chartered Professional Accountant and have spent the last 15+ years in the trenches of small and medium size businesses, watching them shrink, grow, fail and prosper. I myself have also had several businesses over the past 10 years.

Here are the 3 things / concepts that have had the biggest impact on my life personally, professionally and financially:

1. Owning your own business.

Since my days in University when I ran a successful little wedding photography business, I've always been doing some sort of business, and I am still on the journey to create an entity of value that will generational. In the meantime though, there are so many peripheral benefits to owing your own business that are not often talked about.

Here are just a few:

Personal and professional growth

"Ever since I was a child I have had this instinctive urge for expansion and growth. To me, the function and duty of a quality human being is the sincere and honest development of one's potential."

~Bruce Lee

All of us to go school as children, most of us continue to go to school in our youth, and many continue on post-secondary or get educated in a trade. However, when we enter the workplace many people seem to think they are done growing, learning and working on themselves. However, in business you quickly learn that if you don't continue to develop communication skills, leadership qualities and a positive attitude, you won't be around very long. Being in business will offer you challenges that force you to grow and expand if you want to stay in business. For instance, like a typical accountant, I am perfectly happy and most comfortable sitting behind a desk all day. However, I know for my business to grow to the next level, I need to be out in the community meeting people and giving back. Although, it is uncomfortable for me at times, the relationships and connections that I have built are invaluable from a personal and professional standpoint.

<u>Leaving a legacy</u>

"If you would not be forgotten as soon as you are dead, either write something worth reading or do something worth writing."

~ Benjamin Franklin

Building a business is like raising child. In the beginning it is new and there are struggles. You may have to sacrifice sleep and it may be hard to justify the amount of time you are putting when you look at the results. However, like a child, if you continue to nourish and support it in the right way, one day it will take on a life of its own and continue to benefit the community and possibly the world, even after you are gone. For example, at the end of 2014, the Bill & Melinda Gates Foundation had an endowment of approximately $42 billion.

The foundation's primary aim is, globally, to enhance healthcare and reduce extreme poverty, and in the US, to expand educational opportunities and access to information technology. What kind of legacy do you want to leave?

Creativity

"The mere formulation of a problem is far more essential than its solution, which may be merely a matter of mathematical or experimental skills. To raise new questions, new possibilities, to regard old problems from a new angle requires creative imagination and marks real advances in science."

~Albert Einstein

The nature of business lends itself to the creative process. Before you even start a business, your creative juices are already flowing with all the new ideas, possibilities, concepts and opportunities in your mind. In business it take creativity to differentiate you from the competition to stand out, and ultimately succeed. For example, it was reported that, in a one-month span the 2014 the Amyotrophic Lateral Sclerosis (ALS) Association raised almost $100 million through a new initiate called the ice bucket challenge, compared to less than $3 million of donations received during the same time in the prior year.

2. Invest vs. Spend

It was the summer of 2003 when a casual lunch date altered my current reality. That afternoon, my aunt had just mentioned that she purchased two new condo units in downtown Vancouver. At that point, I was aware that the booming housing market in Vancouver and I was very skeptical that it would continue to rising. In fact, I often told myself I would wait for the prices to come down before I thought about buying anything.

"How can you afford to buy two", I asked.

She smiled and replied, "You don't have to pay the whole amount now. You just have to put down a deposit now and pay the rest when you move in...and I will sell them for a profit before they are ready to move into".

"Do you want to take part", she asked.

"Isn't that risky", I replied like a typical accountant.

After listening to my aunt explain all the reasons why she though the prices would keep going up, I was sold. I was saving up some money for a car and a holiday, with a little help from my family, I was able to gather up about $17,000 to get a 1/3 stake in one of the condos and gave it to my aunt before she left and was officially in the real estate game.

A year and a half later, my aunt came back up for another visit to Vancouver and handed me a cheque for $30,000. "The property price went up by 20%, and since we only had to put down a small deposit, our money almost doubled", she explained.

It was at that point, I felt the value of investing vs. spending and the power of leverage.

If I had purchased a car and went on that vacation instead of investing in that first real estate deal with my aunt, it is quite conceivable that I would own no real estate property today.

Instead, I currently own properties in Vancouver, Toronto, Hamilton and Costa Rica.

3. Pay less tax

As a good citizen, I believe that it is our responsibility to pay our fair share of taxes. In Canada we enjoy an amazing standard of living and it is one of the most desirable countries in the world to live in. On a recent trip to China, my father fell and seriously injured his elbow requiring surgery. Although he did initially go to the hospital in China, the standards weren't very comforting and he trekked 3 for three painstaking days to get back to Vancouver get treatment. I know many of us feel like we pay a lot in taxes, and we see a lot of wastage throughout the government, overall we ARE very blessed to living in Canada, and I am proud to be a Canadian!.

However, I also believe that we owe it to ourselves to manage our finances well and take care of the people around us. Therefore, we have a responsibility to keep, in our pockets, as much of the money we earn as possible.

Also, $1 saved in taxes is worth more than $1 extra earned. When you save $1 in tax you keep it. When you earn an extra dollar in income, you may only keep $0.70 after tax.

Here are the top 5 questions that I think EVERYONE should ask themselves. If your answer is "No" or "I don't know" to any of these questions, then it could make a tremendous difference financially for your family to sit down with an accountant to learn more.

1. Some say that there are only two certainties in life – death and taxes. However that is not necessarily the case. In Canada, some things never get taxed. Are you taking advantage of these things?

2. The majority of Canadian's have debt (e.g. a mortgage) and the majority of Canadians have some sort of investment savings. Are you making the most of potential interest deductions for your taxes?

3. Are you doing your best to equalize your family income? If not, you may be giving away money to CRA that you don't have to.

4. Even if you may qualify for a certain tax credits, refunds, and grants, you won't get them unless you ask. Are you maximizing all the available tax credits and refunds and government grants available to you?

5. Do you know how to increase your cash flow without paying more tax? Are you deferring as much of the tax you can now?

Aaron Chan

Aaron Chan has over 10 years of experience in the accounting and financial field. In addition to working with various mid-size CA firms across Canada, Aaron has also spent time as a Canada Revenue Agency auditor, forensic accountant and financial advisor. In his current tax practice, Aaron really enjoys serving small business owners and real-estate investors, as he himself is a passionate entrepreneur. Even during his studies to become a Chartered Accountant, he ran a successful wedding photography business. If he's not in front of his calculator, you'll normally find Aaron enjoying his other passions, playing competitive sports, hanging out with his wife Bonnie at a cool event; or running around in the playground with his two sons Lucas and Jaden.

For a complimentary tax assessment, connect with Aaron at aaron@aaronchan.ca.

www.aaronchan.ca

Cardamon

~

By Aditya Aman

"Sir, how are you feeling now?" asked the police officer, moments after his blue and white car pulled into Credit Valley Hospital; with me in the backseat. I felt like saying "Oh just peachy. Life couldn't get any better! All I need is a red carpet to Heaven to meet God and I'm set"

Ha. That couldn't be further from the truth. You see, I was having an excruciating panic attack at the time. **On face value, my mouth seemed to be making the traditional smile and yet, my brain seemed to be splitting into different directions – all of them heading towards a very dark path.** At the time (circa 2012) Luka Magnotta was on the news and almost coincidentally, I broke up with my girlfriend. If there was one thing **that I wasn't** at that time, it was peace loving, calm and friendly. Oh whether I liked it or not, I had crazy thoughts – towards myself or any other living being. These were thoughts that I could not control apparently.

Now all the above freaked me out big time... I mean I was a simple guy who just wanted simple things, including a simple girlfriend. Not once, had severe uncontrollable thoughts of self-harm or external harm populated my mind before. So by fair logic, I had to call the doc and get checked for my own sake. To accelerate things, they deemed it necessary for me to be chauffeured by a police car.

Huh?

Anyhow, back to the ex-girlfriend and the reason for our breakup.

Let's call her Amy. She was beautiful, homely and had good culture and values – that would make her the ideal wife for a simple Indian guy like myself. We rushed into the relationship really fast and were talking about getting married within a month. I still remember how I felt whenever I heard my phone beep with her texts; that bell sound made my heart so happy. Barely 6 months later, we ended our relationship.

I still don't know why I chose to end it...it baffles me to this day. I thought at the time that it was because she wasn't the one for me. **However, I suspect that it was because I was very unsure of who I was as a person. I didn't know who I was or what I could be and the thought of confining myself as a traditional Indian boy suffocated me.** It was weird because I think I loved her; however I really couldn't picture being with her forever and the reason why still escapes me.

Well, the pain and the trauma from me losing someone close to my heart and boy, was she close…fractured my mind for a little bit there. Even though, it was my own doing and I was the one initiating it. She truly cared for me and was as close to that unconditional female lover archetype as you see in the movies.

So after a night at the hospital, the doc diagnosed me as having extreme anxiety with mild OCD. Wow, well that makes sense I guess?

I always knew I had some feeling of unease trapped in my body, like a goldfish stuck in a leaking bowl of water.

Now we will time travel as they do in the movies to circa 2003. This may help understand my mental makeup.

I was in boarding school in India which while in some ways was a good experience; in other ways was quite horrid. I lost my sense of innocence and security and esteem, especially being picked on by the boys as the fat one who was also gullible. Like icing to the cake; it was pure pudding for some of them. Two years of living there, seemed much longer.

And oh, did I mention? I started having feelings of attractions towards the opposite sex as well. Needless to say, I wasn't the sweet talker or the Brad Pitt incarnate. Add the fact that I was picked on by the boys in my class and yup at the time one would call me repulsive – for the pure reason that I was alive; ha ha! I remember I told this one girl that I liked her (and I really, really did) and her response still rings to me today "It's ok, you can't help it" I mean she was in a league of her own but wow.

I thought I was ringing up Christina Aguilera but actually ended up calling Ann Coulter.

In 2005, I came to Canada to pursue my engineering degree while nursing a broken heart, eroded self-esteem and many other ailments. Add homesickness to that too please. However I ended up not only getting my engineering degree but also made a few great friends; some of whom I still talk to – 12 years later.

My heart though kept enduring rejections from the opposite sex many a time and I feel some of that negativity or should I say **the allure of rejection followed me to other areas too.** In terms of women, I had been rejected so much to the point that I decided to become a hermit…really! In the workplace, I was let go because I couldn't pick up to the pace. In terms of some new friendships, I tried so hard to make people like me – that I would go out of my way to do things for them. To feel loved, appreciated, valued…. **To feel loved, appreciated and valued.** I was so anxious that people wouldn't like me that I would compensate by trying to be the BEST FRIEND ever!! Yeah, that worked very well…NOT.

At a certain point during the above too, I was like Colin Firth's character from the King's Speech. **My anxiety level or fear of being rejected had gotten to a point where I was even afraid to meet people as I would stutter to say, even my name.**

"My name's Eric, what's yours?" "My name is A-a-a-a-a-Aditya" I kid you not, that happened. Not once, twice, thrice…but many times.

…To feel loved, appreciated and valued… that was really what I felt was lacking all this time. This led me to make bad decisions regarding friendships and activities to compensate for the above from 2003 to 2015 or so. Even though my family – my mother, my father and sister did give me love and appreciation always, I felt that I was always missing the same externally. This led to an inbreeding of anxiety inside my spirit which as you could tell came to a high – that fateful night of my breakup. The irony was that she had given me all the above that I wanted but for some reason I couldn't accept it. **Thanks in a way to me feeling comfortable all those years, being under the gun of looking stupid, silly, undervalued, and ridiculous and the "what-have-yous" of being ostracized socially.**

For almost a year and a half after, I lived in a constant state of fear and anxiety of being in the same mental state as I was back in Creditview Hospital. That was until I experienced a shift in my thinking, almost radically.

During all this time, I did have the support of my family as mentioned but more so I fell deeply in love with music and writing. It really gave me a lot of relief to put melody and music from my guitar and marry it with lyrics onto paper. I had developed a bit of writing poetry during my boarding school days, which only served as a precursor to my song writing.

Oh I explored so many avenues with my song writing – be it love, hate, anger, peace, sadness, comfort and many more. I felt free to express my thoughts and feelings as-is, it was a sense of catharsis and purging of my soiled emotions. I have to thank a lot of artists for inspiring me during this time namely The National, The Shins, Nick Cave, Wilco, Interpol and many more.

I figured out around 2014 that hell with the social anxiety; I need to get out there with my music, my ideas and thoughts. Those obviously were one of my main personal strengths that I had developed over the years. I didn't suffer and repress my emotions out of fear and anxiety - just to write to myself, I thought. **Maybe there was someone out there just like me who went through the exact same emotions and what if he/she heard me and felt a little less alone, wouldn't that make the world a better place?**

So I decided to start a new project – called "Beige Shelter". Obviously music served to be my safe spot, my sanctuary, and my shelter with my intent to indulge in music that struck chords in the human spirit – be it sadness, anger, joy and everything else. Beige seemed to be the colour that fit- a peaceful chameleon of sorts.

So I started shyly exploring open mics – starting from the Mississauga Amphitheatre Unplugged at Celebration Square. I remember how nervous I got prior to performing – it literally felt like Niagara Falls from my sweat pores!! But I had to do it; I just knew that I was meant to do something like this, play live and express myself. **I strongly believed that I had a message of hope, resilience, faith and self-reliance from experience, which I wanted to express to others – in the hope of making a difference in the lives of those who may have needed it.**

Well as they say, when you want something so bad – the universe conspires to help you get it. I wanted to release an album. I bumped into my producer and now band mate Neel Modi at a songwriter's meetup and he signed on to do the whole album – "Rumours We Make, Paths We Take" (RWMPWT) which consists of 12 songs. These songs explore various themes such as love, loss, resilience, anxiety and many more. From Oct 2015 – April 2016, we recorded the entire album. The experience was wonderful and I learned the benefits of hiring a good seasoned producer versus my own demos and home recordings – which weren't as appealing as I thought they were.

Right before my album recording was done, I thought to myself "Ok now I have to really, really get out there!" I continued with open mics now at various venues such as The Tilted Kilt, The Cock and Pheasant Bar, The Etobicoke Local – this time with Neel supporting me on percussion.

Just as I was yearning for a complete band, Neel introduced me to Tom Kuczynski – who is one of the most talented bassists/musicians I've ever come across!! Coincidentally I brought one of my young friends: Karan Sabharwal, an extremely talented lead guitarist and voila! Beige Shelter as a band was complete!!

From June 2016 to February 2017, Beige Shelter played at many venues within Toronto and Mississauga such as Lee's Palace (twice), Sneaky Dee's, Clarke Memorial Hall, The Amsterdam Bicycle Club, The Cavern Bar, the Cock and Pheasant Bar, Free Times Café, the Mississauga Multicultural Festival (hosted by James Erdt) and many more. **We have also appeared on the latest DYNAMO Speaker Talent Search 2016 as their musical guest.**

We also released our first single Dark Horse from our album on YouTube (991 views) as well as released RWMPWT electronically on iTunes, Spotify, Google Play and others. **Our Facebook page has 1652 likes, Instagram has 437 followers and one of our Instagram promotions has 16,704 likes!!**

Currently we are preparing for **our physical album CD Release party at The Opera House on March 10** – the Opera House is a prestigious venue and we are honoured to play there. Proceeds from the show are going towards fundraising for the Canadian Mental Health Association – towards the betterment of mental health and awareness! More shows, interviews and appearances to follow later this year! My lesson? Perseverance, faith, passion, humility, compassion, resilience and self-reliance are vital towards making your dreams a reality!

Aditya Aman

Aditya(Adi) Aman is the frontman/lead vocalist/guitarist/ukulelist of an upcoming indie rock band "Beige Shelter" - an ambitious and eclectic indie/ alternative rock band that brings hearts, soul and fire together with its passionate music. He is also a licensed Professional Engineer working in the Transportation Industry . If polygamy was legal, Adi would be married to both engineering and music.. though music would be his favorite wife. He loves supporting social causes including mental heath and awareness, anti-child abuse, anti-domestic abuse, children's education and so on. In his free time, he loves working out, reading, watching movies, spending time with close friends and family, hiking, listening to music (obviously) and also songwriting!

Your Soul Has A Plan For You

~

By Anna DeSantis

You were born with potential.

You were born with greatness.

You were born with wings.

You are not meant for crawling, so don't. – RUMI

So many of us are searching to find ourselves again after decades of abandoning ourselves. We are yearning for connection and meaning, and to love ourselves fully just as we are. Although we truly desire all of this, it can be daunting to begin (and keep going) because the journey to self can be a twisting, turning road with lots of bumps.

A few days before I ended my Twin Flame romantic relationship with a man I loved, to go inside me and do my inner work, I received a message that was something like this:

"So...at the lowest point of our relationship...

At the time when this darkness has peaked...

you have chosen to vacate for your own selfish ends.

I respected you...right up until NOW.

You go do you.

While I go do me."

Now you can imagine despite the many messages from people supporting my journey and loving on me, this one snagged my heart and felt like a punch to my solar plexus. In the two seconds it took to read these six lines I went from a woman about to take a bold action to an insecure little girl full of fearful questions: Am I being selfish? Is it really okay to take care of myself? Am I abandoning everyone? Will I be abandoned in return?

As I breathed into the discomfort in my body, I noticed the voices clambering for attention. Then I went beneath into the silence. The discomfort didn't go away, but now I could see it from a new perspective. I embraced my fears and I want you all to know that FEAR was my gift in that moment. That gift made me smile. It seemed that I was running away from my truth for years. Always looking outside of myself, thinking it was there. As if by magic someone was going to give it to me. As I giggle! Abandoning myself was at the core of what was holding me back from stepping into my truth. So sick of the 9-5 job, I got to a point where I realized there was more for me. I needed to fully love myself and stop abandoning me to discover my truth.

For as long as I can remember, I was so good at illuminating and awakening the souls of others, exposing their true potential and reconnecting them to their heart and pure essence of joy. At the same time, I was so confused as to what my purpose was! Everyone seems to come to me for answers. Then there it was everyone! The answer I was looking for. That's when I decided it was time that I got paid to do this! That's when I COMMITTED to myself. Stop the blaming and look at me. The awareness kicked in and it was all about me. Everyone is me. Disguised! Would you believe it took me over 40 years to figure it out!

What a gift to receive this message of someone's disappointment in me so I could clarify for myself my intent and focus. I plugged myself in, to my essence, my truth, my connection and self-love and there is no going back to the old me.

Here's the thing, dear ones:

When you are living your truth and centering yourself in the starry sky of your authenticity, you are going to disappoint, piss off, upset, and freak out some people.

If you are not, it means you are placating, care taking, and tip toeing around conflict. And that is no way to live. I was over the virtue trap as I discuss in one of my online courses. It was painful and I couldn't pretend any longer. Now, I'm not saying go out and upset people on purpose. I'm saying BE YOU. Let others BE THEMSELVES. Being YOU is inspiring you, to shine your light from your HEART, not EGO, and create the change that you want to see. That's when I started to shelve the ego though still loving my ego.

Because here is what it comes down to: I get to make the choices that feel right for me, and others get to like or not like, support or judge, celebrate or dismiss me.

I respect their choice. Even when they don't respect mine. Because whatever anyone says about me IS NONE OF MY BUSINESS. My energy is focused in my heart space.

This is what I feel is missing today.

Would you believe, I took the harder road. I went inside of myself to birth the real me and gift my super awesomeness to the world. I came here to be in 100% service. To shine the light and unconditionally love. The most important relationship is the one you have with yourself. I learnt how to develop self love and connect with my true essence.

So, in my ascension journey and recognizing the truth of who I am and why I came to Earth, I now have a better understanding of this:

It is much easier to match anger with anger, blame with blame, hurt with hurt. That was an old way of BE-ing and showing up in my life. Once I stopped running away from me, life started to happen. The people, places and things started to show up as if by magic. As I started to connect with my Higher Self, my life became an effortless expression of JOY. My joy is the gift I gift the billions of you on earth. I heard the quiet voice of inspiration inside of me, but felt overwhelmed with the idea of taking the spiritual journey because I was afraid that if I showed up as the real ANNA that I would be judged. Crazy! What was I thinking!! I realized that I am the gift and nothing was going to stop me. That's when I committed myself to ME.

Now, I am asking you all to carry a mirror with you for one week, an imaginary mirror. Before you speak to anyone, first observe, and then place the mirror in front of them as if you are speaking to yourself. The truth is, we are all information, and mirror whatever needs to come up within ourselves through others. Everyone is a gift. And if you ever need clarity as to where you are, look at what is showing up in your current reality. If you don't like what you see, this is when you go inside and work with your 'stuff'.

Please be brave, and compassionate, and curious.

Ask questions. Take action based on your beliefs.

Respect everyone.

Even when you don't agree with them.

Especially when you don't agree with them.

This is the road less traveled: going into stillness to shift from reaction to conscious response. Being willing to see someone else's point of view even if you absolutely, 100% believe it is wrong. Telling yourself the truth. Being willing to be wrong. Being willing to be right. Being willing to stand up for what you love.

Be an activist of the heart, rather than from fear.

I'm in for the good fight, for the long haul. That fight is for awareness, presence, love, honesty, compassion, creativity, curiosity, wisdom, authenticity and respect. That fight is about doing our own inner work as we also take action in the outer world. That work is shaking ourselves awake from passivity and powerlessness and following what we are passionate about. That work is about weaving together our human commonality instead of creating more fear-based divisions.

I'm here to help foster a community of love, to help build a tidal wave of consciousness, to build bridges of awareness and respect. Because we are in this together.

Here are some ways to stay engaged and informed:

I. Remember, baby steps.

2. Don't feed into the negativity and fear. Listen from your heart and act from your beliefs seeped in a connection to the silence that underlies all the noise.

3. Always be grateful for everything and everyone, everyday.

If we wish to know ourselves, we must, not neglect but embrace the wholeness of who we are. This is inclusive of the 'dark stuff' that bothers us. Love your journey. Love everything that shows up in your life. Only then can we see the world from a perspective of inclusivity and courage.

Again, your life is just a mirror. So when you put your attention on those things that you're passionate about and then when you start to align with those things, what you find is the doors start to open. In order to change the external world, first we must change within ourselves.

'At the end of the day, it's not about what you have or what you've accomplished. It is about what you have done with these accomplishments. It's about who you've lifted, who you have made better. It is about what you have given back.'

– Denzel Washington

Are you feeling called to play a bigger role in your work and the world, as a conscious feminine leader? Are you seeking to unleash your full potential in alignment with and in service to your Higher Self? Are you ready to birth your gift to the world and ditch the 9-5 job? I would be honored to be your midwife and ignite within you, your wholeness, peace and creativity. Are you ready to transform virtually every aspect of your life?

That's my gift. Together we will transform self doubt, get you into living and leading in more consistent alignment with your gifts and calling, transform challenges that feel personal into a committed stand to make a difference and to lead with clarity, power and feminine flow. I will help you discover YOUR authentic leadership. I will guide you into your deep reservoir of inner wisdom and into leading a more organic, connected, conscious and joy-filled way from your highest guidance. That's it everyone, that voice within you, that's your Higher Self, that's your truth, start to listen to your Higher Self, let go of this physical body and ego thinking. You're Higher Self is trying to get your attention so that you can fully step into service. Stop running from it like I did for over 40 years. Allow me to guide you, and plug you in to the REAL YOU so you can step fully into your inspired leadership, so you can start to co-create profound positive impacts in the world. Remember purity of heart and purity of intent creates the flow through your vehicle. The world needs your gift.

I love you all and thanks to all whom believe and support my journey. What else is possible?

Anna DeSantis

Anna DeSantis

Sacred Soul Blueprint Midwife

Divine Channel of love and light In-Joy

Goddess of Light Blue Ray Oraphim

Ascension Guide, Quantum Alchemist, Visionary, Speaker

www.rawkstarleaders.com

goddess-anna (instagram)

Anna, enables clients to accelerate their awakened consciousness and reach higher levels of spiritual enlightenment. Participants regularly experience deep healing along with an abundance of life force, all while releasing limited programs and energy patterns, fears and belief systems that have long blocked their well-being and self-realization. Anna is committed to accessing higher levels of human potential while teaching and ever improving upon her techniques for personal evolution and self-realization. Born and raised in Toronto, Canada.

Anna is available for consultations and speaking engagements and can be reached by contacting via her webpage.

I've Been On A Mission

~

By Anne Gagnon

Today when I look back, I remember how sickly I was for most of my young life. When I was old enough to understand, my adoptive mother would tell me that the day I arrived in the family, she could not believe the many ailments I had. It was difficult for her to care for me, I was allergic to most foods, my diet was limited, and every inch of my skin was affected. She would apply cortisone cream from my head to my toes; I remember her saying how expensive it was. Stressful times for a family with 2 teen age boys and a sick child with no my birth family health history.

Growing up in the country with apple orchards surrounding our property, the amazing scent of beautiful apple blossoms was something I never experienced – I stayed home from school during that time – the allergies were so severe before my teen years, I would be home more than at school. Sometimes, not very often, I would go to the grocery store with my mom and 2 aisles before the fruits and vegetables, I would go to the cash register and wait for her.

If we didn't do that, within 5 minutes, I'd end up with the redress, most swollen and scary looking eyes you've ever seen, my whole respiratory system would almost shut down, felt like I was chocking and my sinuses got so blocked, I could not breathe. My mother had a drug store in her purse in case something happened, it was terrible, and I was constantly putting medication in my eyes, my nose and my mouth to get some relief.

When I was 11 years old, still as sick, and fragile, they took me for allergy testing – after several hours, my arms, legs and back had been poked and scratched, they determined that I was basically allergic to almost everything… and that I would need 2 shots a week to help with my condition. So every Friday after school, the doctor would give me a needle in each arm. That went on for over a year and I still was the same; why am I not getting better?

In my mid-teens, sickly and a loner, I read a lot and I very much enjoyed subjects like health, how the body worked, I thought I might like to become a doctor to help the sick. I admired Mother Theresa and wanted to start my own mission of helping people. I was so tired of being sick all the time, I often felt depressed but I had to keep going.

I started questioning; with all the medications that I've been administered since a baby how come I'm still sick? I did a lot of research at the library, continued reading and searching for the answers, and as I got closer, I found Dr. Linus Pauling and vitamin C. I discovered things like homeopathy, herbs and different therapies that helped people with their ailments, I was fascinated and hungry to discover that I could potentially have the answer to help my situation.

One thing for sure, I didn't have enough vitamin C in my diet, I never ate fruits or veggies, I was allergic and citrus were the worst, so I recall running to the pharmacy to look for some type of compound. I started taking 500mg of vitamin C every morning and continued reading and learning and within about a month, something was happening, I felt encouraged!

That's when things started to change! I realized that I was 'under-nourished' and when I introduced missing elements to my body, I was now able to 'feed' my nutrient starving cells to finally achieve a higher sense of health and wellness.

Then, the biggest shock of our lives, daddy is diagnosed with cancer at 59. Went into the hospital before Christmas and never came home. Surgery, radiation, more surgery, complications, more drugs, surgery, and then after the chemo ended, he died, and 3 months shy of his 60th birthday.

I will never forget that day, I said to my mother "I will find out why daddy died, it's not right for people to suffer like he did – I'm on a mission, I'm going to find out why he got so sick".

For the next 5 years I continued reading and getting healthier, feeding myself well, taking my vitamin supplements, my body was tolerating more food, my allergies weren't as severe, I knew I was on to something and remembered these important words of wisdom by Hippocrates "let food be thy medicine and medicine be thy food." That's when I knew, for me, drugs were not the answer.

My health was getting much better, life was good! I was married and happy, I was 32, had a great pregnancy and gave birth to a beautiful healthy boy, my pride and joy! With this new responsibility it became paramount that I know exactly how to care for my baby and my mission got even bigger and I was fortunate to get more help! The Internet arrived! And I thank God to this day that I had an amazing supportive partner, we transformed into environmentalists!

No IPads, my bedside books were Earl Mindell's "Vitamin Bible" and "You're not sick you're Thirsty" by Dr. Batmanghelidj or as I call him, Dr. Batman! We had a small garden, I cooked all our food from scratch just like my mother did. I would watch documentaries on the environment, information about food, and how things get processed and ready for consumption – anything about health would be at the front of my mind all the time.

I discovered so many nuggets like 'pier reviewed published clinical studies' and even researched the protocol and importance of these studies, so important! I purchased every book I thought would help me in my quest – I even worked in a health food store to get even more exposure!

I became fascinated when I found out that the simple herb Turmeric, had thousands of years of use with amazing results for inflammation and so many more disorders ever replacing certain allopathic medicines! Plus there are over 5000 'pier reviewed published clinical studies'!

I'm now educating through seminars and private consultation, also still researching, reading, discovering and learning. Over the past few decades, I've been able to help families find a new lifestyle and a real path to wellness! It warms my heart when they do well. New science emerges and I feel I must share the new discoveries that will help humanity, I need to transmit the message that taking care of our health is our responsibility.

7 years ago I did exactly that – took my health in my own hands – I was diagnosed with rheumatoid arthritis in my right hand and the Dr. said I would need anti-inflammatory drugs and pain killers – well I decided against the treatment. I started researching and found an amazing book by Dr. Theodore Baroody, Alkalize or Die – written in 1981 – and the answer was in the first paragraph of the book.

My arthritis was due to acid waste buildup (or oxidative stress – discussed a bit later) in my joints and plus I was dehydrated – I needed to detox, hydrate and alkalize my tissues, had to find ways for better elimination by eating more fiber and by consuming more alkalizing forming foods, there was some relief. Along with essential oils, Turmeric, and food supplements, I felt 50% better.

Then a colleague introduced me to electrolyzed reduced water and explained that he had a technology that created 'hydrogen-rich' water which was extremely beneficial – the water could detox at the cellular level, could also hydrate at the cellular level because of the structure – I immediately wanted to drink some! I remembered reading about Hydrogen Therapy as a new science about 10 years ago so I was very excited to find out more. Used in many clinics around the world, this technique has helped thousands of people.

When it comes to drinking water, molecular hydrogen has been scientifically proven to be the therapeutic touch our bodies need for the deepest, quickest form of detoxification and the strongest antioxidant on the planet. You can't eat enough antioxidant-rich food in a day to come close to that of the power of the anti-oxidant properties of hydrogen. Our brains, organs, bones and tissues require it!

This mission started 42 years ago when my dad died of cancer – I discovered that he suffered with what Dr. Tim McKnight studied a lot, 'oxidative stress' which is the damage made to a cell through the oxidative process. In itself, a normal process, it happens all the time to our bodies and many things that surround us. When there are disturbances in the natural oxidation process, the results are often toxic effects. The body cannot eliminate and the toxins keep flowing through the body tissues.

The other Dr. I found during my research was awarded the 1931 Nobel Prize in Medicine. Dr. Otto Heinrich Warburg, got the prize for his discovery of the nature and mode of action of the respiratory enzyme. He has shown, among other things that cancerous cells can live and develop, even in the absence of oxygen – cancer cannot live in an oxygenated environment.

Modern medicine has found ways for us to live longer, yet our quality of life, especially during the last 35 years or so, has gone down. This can be attributed to oxidative stress and the toxins that we're encountering more and more throughout our lives. To date, science has discovered that oxidative stress may very well be the cause of over 60 well known widely spread diseases.

Depending on what form of toxin or stress the body is exposed to on an ongoing basis, you could find yourself suffering, even at an early age, from diseases that could be prevented if only you'd have minimized the harmful free radicals in your system. That's what happened to me with the rheumatoid arthritis!

I've listed a few of these diseases here: Cancer – heart disease – arthritis – diabetes – autoimmune disease – the list goes on – I can be found in Dr. Baroody's book Alkalize or Die

I'm now 62 years young, I feel like a million bucks! I've been living an awesome lifestyle, I've been drinking restructured water for 7 years, and so has my family and one thing I can say honestly, I've never felt better, I never get sick and now I know why and how it's possible to achieve a higher sense of wellness. A very important thing I learned over the years has to do with household cleaning and disinfecting products – most of them are extremely toxic and can really damage the health of a whole family without them ever suspecting.

My mission is turning into a commitment to help educate as many people as possible, to respect nature and help the environment as best I can. If it was made in a plant, perhaps think twice before consuming it! If it comes from a God given plant; enjoy and eat it with pleasure! To Your Wellness!

Anne Gagnon

Anne Gagnon is as a health advocate who helps and guides people to wellness. She offers education and lifestyle awareness through seminars and workshops. She was an extremely sickly baby, child and up to her late teens, always at the doctor's office, always on different medications – a terrible time and not long after that, as a very young woman, she lost my father to a preventable lifestyle related disease. That very day, she started on a mission to educate herself on prevention and wellness and that has led her through over 40 years of amazing discoveries. Wellness and disease prevention have become a real passion and the more she discovers, the more she realizes, she needs to share this awareness with the world. One of the most important aspect of wellness is hydration and now she has focused her energies on educating about our drinking water choices.

Anne Gagnon 647-864-8694

WaterHealth4Life@gmail.com

www.WaterHealth4Life.com

The Secret is to Give and Receive

~

By Dr. Elio Franco Filice

To whom the wisdom is for, you will know. Be one with one, he who is one with one will know all that he will need to know. Knowledge that is for one is for all, knowledge for all is for one. There is no all and there is no one. To remember is to forget is to remember. To feel is to be physical to enjoy, live, and to love. Words of wisdom are simple and are true for the meaning is within and between the words the tool is yours to have.

During the journey the love of self and others is most important. Compassion with dedication to your work is the secret. Through love of self and others true service occurs. It is our service to others that we strive for in our lives. To serve others comes in many forms and becomes our vocation. We will know what our purpose will be when our passion and service to others coincide. Service to others need not be grandiose, only to be done in love and with commitment. For when we truly serve will we be congruent in life, enjoy happiness, health and prosperity.

Our obstacles will become the fire for us to transform and find our purpose and way at that moment. Life is meant to be lived, not to be existed. When we fulfill our destiny though our work, relationships and community do we come alive. There will always be ups and downs for we are always learning and through our learning's do we become who we are meant to be.

We grow through our experiences. If we continue to do the same every day we may lose our way. To start every day with fresh eyes will help motivate and create the day for ourselves. There are times when we are not ourselves and requesting the help of others is not a failure but an act of strength. It is through partnership with another person that we can grow our resources for both. Be it emotional resources or physical or financial.

The secret is to both give and receive. If we only ever give and not allowing ourselves to receive, even if it means taking five minutes just to sit and relax in silence, we will lose sight of the prize, of our purpose. It is also through receiving that we feel fulfilment. To receive what is given to us with gratitude. To say thank you to life, to your spouse, mate, children, whomever and whatever, for the gifts given to us. Begin and end the day in gratitude. There will be days where you may find it difficult to see the gifts but they are there, you only need to receive them with gratitude.

Create the life you want by placing your focus on it. Visualize it, feel and hear it. Then begin to act as you already have it. Behave the way you would in your ideal life. If you to be athletic then move your body, do not sit in front of your television and only wish and talk about it.

As we live life we encounter stuff, and that is all it is- stuff. How we deal with our stuff is what creates the obstacle or the opportunity.

Through focused action we can transform the stuff into what we want at the time. As with any learned process with repetition we become more proficient, more confident with the process. So will dealing with stuff. We must avoid labeling it as good or bad as such terms are limiting. We will have emotions with the stuff as we are humans having a physical experience. We are meant to cry, get angry, laugh, love- too Feel. We are not computers without emotions rather computers with emotions. We learn as a computer learns though pattern recognition such as the typing features on our smartphones. Our experiences are our patterns. As we experience and live life does our computer-like brain process and builds on it. Our emotions also help us build our programs and interactions with others.

As we learn we move forward. We can plan ahead. And as we learn, patterns will change, our experience will change and so will our plan. The more flexible we are the more we can create, more we live, and the more we create. Life is a circle of self-creation consciously or unconsciously. We cannot stop to action. Dreaming, imagining who and what we are is one part of the process. We must do, act, reassess and be flexible enough to change in midcourse. To expect to always be in one state is not possible. In physics what goes up comes down. There are laws in physics that keep our physical world never ending. Energy transforms to matter and back to energy. It is a cycle. So are we, evolving and changing every day, every year into a new you. Why not create the you with intent rather than unconsciously and with happenstance.

When we act with our eyes open we can see the opportunities that present themselves to us. We are aware of them no matter what, and though that awareness we can act. Initially the changes and manifestations in the new you are not always visible to you or others. As time progresses the accomplishments of you in the past moments become evident.

Life is wonderful in that we never know what the future holds so that we can imagine and dream as we act to make it happen. Opportunities always present that are for your benefit and for the benefit of others. If stuff arises that appears to be an opportunity but is not of benefit to you or others or both then it is not an opportunity and walk away.

As we act for both our own benefit and those of others will your life change and that of the world. We can change the world by only acting when the benefits are yours and that of others. One small step or as it may appear to be by one person, when added to all who act for the benefit of self and others will it lead to massive change. Do not focus on actions that are not of benefit to yourself or others. As we live our lives with intent in whatever we do will then the change begin to occur. If you are a physician acting to help change the health of another or selling candy at a corner store it matters not when acting for self and others. It matters not if you run a $700 billion company or a $700 dollar company as it is this congruent action of benefit to all that will move us.

Today marks the day of your transformation, great masters have come and gone in all walks of life. Your learning's are all around you for you to find to create the life you long for within. Take each day to visualize, act out in your imagination, in your quiet openness of mindfulness. Ideas will come for you to act upon. Grand or not is for you to determine. As children we playfully create our day playing endlessly imagining possibilities. Do not limit your possibilities for they are endless. We seek to live a grandiose life for that is what we are told. And it will be grandiose in the eyes of the beholder-you. Do not feel guilt for following your path as it is yours to set. Mine has been wondrous for me. Be committed to who you are and the love you share.

Move and continue to move, for movement though life is what creates. Giving back to community throughout your journey is very important. Be it a smile to a stranger or helping rebuild homes and lives.

Whatever giving back is for you follow it.

Continue to learn the skills of your chosen path. As you learn optimization not perfection is the key. Begin to share; teaching others your learning's and skills. Mentorship allows creativity to continue. As you gain the knowledge of creativity sharing creation is transformational. Sharing and receiving are simultaneous when living in joy and with purpose.

Discovering your purpose, your why will guide your actions. For action without purpose is not very effective. Focused action from purpose and your why will lead to wonderful results. For some discovering your purpose, your why will be easy and effortlessly and for others it will be as hard as they want it to be now. There may be times we may lose our way, begin to behave from what we do rather then why we are doing it.

As we discover new paths, new avenues to take, if we journey them with our purpose and why in mind and in our hearts we will be limitless. Potential does not come in a pill, or from someplace or someone, it comes from within. When you feel stuck, not able to move look for help from others that have taken the journey. Let them be your GPS to bring you back to your path and journey. To become lost and aimlessly search for the road may lead to a place we did not want to be at all. Stop, take a moment and ask for directions. Do not use all your energy searching for your way. Continuing to take a right turn will only lead you back to where you started. To be independent and strong are good traits to have and learning to be interdependent with other people is also required.

Remember to have fun. As children we played and learned simultaneously. A life skill that is best kept for life. Look not at those around you and gauging their accomplishments for it will only distract you. Focus on your journey and your purpose and what you seek will find you and will be yours.

We all cross the finish line at some point and we also leave this earth with what we entered. The speed to the finish line is not the prize for the journey is the prize.

You have all the answers with you. You need only to have the courage to seek and find them. Let yourself be guided and guide yourself, for when you let go of control do you ultimately have control. Control is an illusion, what you have is free will, the freedom to choose what you want and to create it. Water moves gracefully and unencumbered as the earth appears not to move. The fluidity of water guides it to where it needs to be and so our fluidity will guide us. Work within natures laws. I have not written what I do for my purpose with these words are not the what but to guide. We all need guidance from time to time and I have been guided to contribute these words. For some these words will resonate and for others it will not have much meaning. These words are not for all but for those who want to create their journey. Your belief in being the creator of your journey is the start. Embrace it, nurture the belief. Begin to take baby steps if you have not begun to consciously pursue your journey. Research, read, pursue learning experiences to discover your purpose and your why. Once you have your purpose and the why the how you want to create your journey. You may find that what you are doing at this moment will not change for you. You may find more fulfilment and joy in what you are doing as the awareness of your why and how arises. You may also find that what you are doing is no longer for you and your journey will take you to developing a new what for you to accomplish. Be wise, patient and open to your journey. Do not abandon your life but allow it to evolve. Become the master and captain of your evolution. We are constantly evolving consciously or unconsciously so why not chose which way. Consciously chose and create your evolution, an evolution full of splendour and adventure of your creating. A soulful evolution guided by you though your choices and actions. Give thanks to our creator for allowing us the gift of free will. Free to create who we want to become, an evolution of self that will bring out your magnificence and is of betterment for everyone.

The choice is yours, choose wisely. Thank you for reading these words and pages.

Dr. Elio Franco Filice

Dr. Elio Filice has devoted over 28 years of his professional life to the practice of dentistry. His devotion is to help others achieve the level of oral health they are seeking in a proactive and involved manner. Dr. Filice begins the process of establishing oral health by forming relationships and partnering with his patients.

For further information visit www.filicedental.com

The 5 Steps To Achieving Anything You Want!
~

By Frank D'Urzo

Life for most people can be extremely complicated and very overwhelming. The stresses of your career, relationship, family and lifestyle can lead you to a place where you feel overwhelmed and "stuck"; stuck in a place where you are not motivated and uninspired to move forward with anything.

Over the years I have discovered that less is more and if you keep things simple, you can make the changes that are necessary for you to succeed at whatever it is you desire. This will require you to begin truly being honest with yourself. It will take some time, patience, probably some money, and definitely some effort. By following the next 5 steps I can guarantee that YOU can achieve anything you want and very likely, even more!

1. WHAT is it that you want?

This seems like such a simple question, but I can't tell you how many people struggle to answer this question. People are always very clear with what they don't want, but never really put all that much thought into what they do want. Here is a little secret, you will get what you ask for in life! If you are constantly telling yourself what you don't want, it is more than likely you will get more of what you don't want. Ask yourself what it is that you really want. This is a very important question as this will be the foundation for everything. You will not be able to move forward unless you know the answer to this question. Knowing what you want gives you a target to focus on. Without this you will find yourself wandering aimlessly trying to figure out why you are not progressing in life.

Usually the most popular answer is, "I just want to be happy!" Well that isn't enough. You are a human being and it is impossible to be happy all the time. Being happy for the most part is definitely the ultimate goal for all of us and I'm going to tell you, being happy is easy. Happy is the feeling you get as a result of the progress you are making in your life. Happy is the feeling you get when things are achieved and happy is the feeling you get when you are receiving love.

"When you trade your expectations for appreciation your world will change instantly." -Anthony Robbins

There are people who are living below the poverty line in North America and there are people in developing countries who are happy because they appreciate simple things. They find happiness in what they have such as family and friends. With all that being said, take some time to figure out what it is that you do want. This may take a little soul searching on your part. You will have to get in touch with who you really are and what you really like. You may have to go back to your younger days and remember the things you used to really enjoy doing or you may want to look at yourself in the mirror and ask yourself what are things you would like to accomplish in the near future.

During this process, make a list of all the things you do want. When you are writing this list remember to be honest and realistic with yourself. As you continually make progress you will have to update and maybe revise your list. Review your list everyday as it will constantly keep you focused on the things you do want.

Determining what you want is so important because when you get the things you want, it will make you happier, it will make you have that sense of pride and you will see yourself in a whole new light!

Have fun with this! Imagine how you will feel like when you get what you want. What will you be saying to yourself and what will other people be saying to you? Picture it, what will you look like when you have the things you want?

2. WHY do you want it?

Now that you know WHAT you want, the next step is to determine WHY you want it!

Why do you want these things? This can't be a simple answer, your why has to be BIG! This has to be so important to you that it will excite you or this may have to be something that really upsets you. You know that you have to do something about it. It has to be something that you are extremely passionate about to ensure it is addressed. Sometimes it's about proving people wrong or proving to yourself that you can accomplish whatever you want.

"When you know why you do what you do, even the toughest days become easier!" -Eric Thomas

This will be your motivation and inspiration when things start to get a little difficult or downright hard. Your why is what will get you out of bed in the morning and keep you up late at night, even when you are tired. Your why is going to make sure you keep going no matter what obstacles get in your way. You may have to really dig deep to discover your why because your why has to be bigger than your Why Not! Why is it so important you get what you want? If you can answer this question whole heartedly then you will be able to get what you want.

"Others have seen what is and asked why, I've seen what could be and asked why not?" -Pablo Picasso

3. HOW can you get it?

Now you have your WHAT and your WHY, the next step is HOW? Ask yourself how can I get what I want? Currently there are people who already have what you want. How did they get it? How did they put themselves in a position to have what you want? As you continuously ask yourself, "How can I?", more and more ideas will start to come to mind.

Subconsciously you are programming your mind to constantly look for the answers to the questions you ask yourself. So if you keep asking yourself, "How did I get myself in this position?" guess what, you will get that answer and remain in the exact same position you are in. When you start to ask yourself "How can I?", your brain will give you the answers you need to move forward! You will find yourself searching different things on the internet, watching different things on TV, and reading different books and articles. You may also find yourself taking new courses, joining new groups and associating with many different people. All of these different resources will be in alignment and they will all guide you closer and closer to what it is that you want.

4. TAKE ACTION!

Once you have established your WHAT, your WHY and your HOW, then you must start to take action and ask yourself, what am I willing to do to get what I want? This is a very important question because this is where you will separate yourself from everybody else. Those who are willing to make sacrifices in their life and start doing what they say they are going to do, are the ones who actually achieve what they want. Going after what you want will take time, money and energy, so what and how much are you willing to give up to get it? You can go after it with everything you got or you can take a gentler approach to it. Either way is okay, as long as you are taking action.

Ask yourself, in the next 24 to 48 hours what can I do to get me closer to what I want? It doesn't have to be a huge step forward, but it definitely has to be something that will get you moving. Take one small step in the direction towards the things you want and this will start to create momentum for you. There will be some challenges in the beginning and that is to be expected because you are stepping into an unfamiliar place which can be uncomfortable. Don't worry, it is okay to feel uncomfortable. Be patient with yourself as you are taking steps to achieve your new goals.

"If you want to change, then you have to be willing to be uncomfortable." -Unknown

You may now have a different mindset around this and you are okay with being uncomfortable because you have your WHY. This will keep you going no matter what obstacles you face. Taking action speaks volumes for your self-esteem and as you continue, you will achieve small victories along the way. This will create more and more momentum. Once the momentum begins for you it will be very difficult for anything to get in your way of success. The more action you take, the more you will learn. When you combine learning and action you will be unstoppable!

5. REWARD YOURSELF!

You are working hard, you are seeing progress and you are getting closer and closer to what you want. Your why is driving you and you are constantly asking yourself, how can I? You are getting the answers you need and the right people are in your life now. Staying focused and chasing what you want will take a bit out of you physically and mentally, so it is very important that every once in awhile you take a break to look back and see how far you have come. Pat yourself on the back, reward yourself by doing something that will allow you to refresh yourself physically and mentally. Do something that is relaxing and allow your body and brain to rest. Watch a funny movie, go for a walk, get a way for a day, do something that will allow you to unwind so that you can feel refreshed.

Remind yourself, your hard work has been appreciated and you deserve the reward. When you are physically and mentally refreshed you will be more motivated and inspired to reach for more. Remember, even God took a day off when he created the world!

To your success!!!

Frank

Frank D'Urzo

Frank D'Urzo is a Motivational Speaker, Master Life Coach and Trainer of NLP. He is very passionate about living life to its fullest and works with men and women who are stuck in the overwhelm of life.

After battling through his own trials and tribulations of divorce; the feelings of pain, stress, anxiety, depression and overwhelm really took a toll mentally and physically on Frank. After enough was enough Frank looked at himself in the mirror and made a decision to change his life. Since then he has transformed himself from and out of shape individual to an endurance athlete. He lost over 30lbs and became a frequent competitor in marathons and Ironman triathlons.

Frank has worked with several of the top personal development trainers in North America and has studied under Anthony Robbins Research. He is a board certified Master Practitioner and Trainer of Neuro Linguistic Programming. He continues to educate himself extensively in personal development, psychology, neuroscience and business.

He has now dedicated his life to inspiring others through his words and his actions. He continually shares his story and knowledge of personal transformation, so that others can be their best selves as well.

It Hasn't Always Been This Way

~

By Joel Martin

The last few years have been the most successful of my career – tripling my income, buying a house alone in my 20s, releasing my 12th album, creating some of the biggest events in my city and becoming a judge for the Juno Awards. Things haven't always been this way.

I started my career in the entertainment industry at age 16, when I released my first album. I then spent the next 12 years barely making rent, not having enough money to buy groceries for several days at a time and sleeping in my car in the middle of winter while on tour. I vividly remember waking up in the middle of the night and trying to take a sip from my water bottle only to realize that it was frozen solid.

My greatest gift proved to be my perseverance. I was willing to experience the absolute lowest of lows in the pursuit of the future I wanted to create for myself. That allowed me to hold on to my dream long enough to develop some real musical talent, to develop my business acumen and to surround myself with a network of entertainment industry professionals. As Jim Carrey famously said "You can fail at what you don't want so you might as well take a chance on doing what you love".

There have been many great lessons I've learned on this incredible journey. If I could only share my 3 biggest insights with the next generation, it would be these:

1. You will be paid in direct proportion to the skills you've developed and the amount of value that you offer others.

I once heard a story that perfectly captures the lack of self-awareness that most people have and their struggles to find a suitable career. It went something like this.

There's a woman and her father out for a walk downtown when suddenly the father starts having a heart attack and falls to the ground. The women calls out for help and a crowd gathers. A man approaches and says that he can help. She asks if he's a doctor and he responds that he isn't but that he's a nice guy. She tells him "that's great, but how does that help me? I really need a doctor!" The man persists, saying that he's not a doctor, but that he's always on time and his friends can count on him. She tells him that he seems like a nice guy who's trustworthy and reliable, but that doesn't help her right now as her father is having a heart attack and she just really needs a doctor. The man walks away feeling rejected and wondering why she denied his offer to help.

The moral of the story is that when it comes to having a career and generating income, the skills you have and the value you offer are what dictate your success. The man in the story couldn't understand why, despite being a nice guy and having other positive attributes, he wasn't in demand. He simply didn't have any skills that could offer value to the situation. That is where most people fall short and lack self-awareness. I know many people who have great qualities but haven't developed any skills. They make great friends but are completely unemployable. If you can't identify exactly what it is that you offer, you will never be able to sell yourself in a job interview.

There's a reason why an employee at McDonald's will make minimum wage, a doctor will make 6 figures a year and Beyonce will make millions. The McDonald's employee can easily be replaced with virtually anyone to take over his or her position. The doctor has acquired knowledge, has developed a skill-set and is capable of doing things that most people cannot. As a result, he or she is paid more. There's only one Beyonce and she cannot be replaced, which is why she makes millions. She developed her talent, built her brand and offers tremendous value to others.

2. You need to learn financial literacy and take the fate of your financial future into your own hands.

They don't teach financial literacy in schools. Is it any surprise that most of the population is in debt and struggling just to get by? We're not taught how to generate income, how to keep it once we've acquired it, and how to leverage it to generate more income. The goal is not to accumulate money for the sake of accumulating money. Money is just the currency that is used to buy freedom and we accumulate it to be able to spend the rest of our lives doing the things that make us come alive. Life is too short to spend your best days working to make someone else rich while you make just enough to get by.

The first step is to stop believing all the negative connotations that you've heard growing up, like "money is the root of all evil", "money doesn't grow on trees" and that all rich people have acted unethically to gain their wealth. Start seeing money as freedom, power and leverage. Realize that money is just the currency that allows us to look after our families, to have the freedom to pursue our dreams and the resources to help make a difference in the world on a bigger scale. If you're struggling financially, you're not in much of a position to help others, as you can barely help yourself. However, someone like Anthony Robbins with a net worth of hundreds of millions of dollars has the power and leverage to set up an initiative to feed 100 million families and Bill Gates with a net worth of $85 billion has donated $28 billion to enhance healthcare and reduce extreme poverty. The first step in changing your financial future is to cleanse your negative associations with money and replace them with positive ones. You attract that which you love and understand. If you hate money, if you fear money and if you want nothing to do with it... you'll never have any.

The second step is to pay yourself first and then spend from whatever is left. Most people spend and then save if there is anything left over. What I mean by "pay yourself first" is: as soon as you receive money, take out a specific amount to put into savings before you spend any of it. Let's be honest. For most people, if they have money, they'll find a way to spend it. This means that when someone says they'll save money if there's any left at the end of the month, there will rarely be anything left to save. If you pay yourself first, however, you'll learn to live off of whatever is left. The easiest way to make this happen is to have a predetermined amount automatically taken from every paycheque and put into a savings account. What amount should automatically be taken off of every paycheque? Minimum: 10%. If you get a $1000 paycheque, have $100 automatically deposited into a savings account then live off of the remaining $900. Let's do the math here. 26 paycheques a year x $100 is $2600 automatically put into the savings account. If you work 45 years from the time you're 20 until you retire at the average age of 65, that's $117,000. That does not include compound interest, saving more than the minimum 10% or the raises to your salary that you'll inevitably receive as you further develop your skills and offer more value to others. If you take the last example and add compound interest at the average rate in Canada of 6%, you'll have $586,321 in savings when you retire. What makes this even more astonishing is that we're using someone with a salary of under $30,000 a year for this example. If you're making $60,000 or $100,000 a year, your savings will be in the millions. Having $100 taken off every paycheque won't really be noticed, and I guarantee that having 6 to 7 figures in your bank account upon retirement will. If you're starting this habit in your 30s or 40s, that's ok, you'll just have to put aside a bigger amount every month.

The final step is to spend your money on assets and not on liabilities. The average person is spending their money on restaurants, movies, expensive TV channel packages and video games, for example. That's money they'll never get back. Spend your money on assets that will not only make your money back, but that will continue to make you money into the future. Instead of spending $1000 on a Backstreet Boys meet and greet, invest in a guitar and lessons. With practice you can develop enough skill to offer value to others and generate income by providing guitar lessons, doing live performances and releasing albums. Other examples: you could learn a new language, take dance lessons or cooking classes... all with the goal of turning around and using those new skills to provide value to others and get paid in return. Certain larger purchases such as a car or a house can sometimes be seen as liabilities, but in my case they're assets. The tenants that live in my house put over $20,000 a year in passive income into my pockets. Not only do I live rent-free but my mortgage is also 100% being paid off by others. That's an asset. If you normally spend 2 hours a day (40 hours a month) using public transit, purchasing a used car at a fair price – which in turn cuts your commute time in half – can prove to be extremely valuable. If you use those 20 hours that you get back to do things that generate income, that car will quickly pay for itself and then some.

3. Happiness can only truly be found when it is shared.

I spent most of my life ruthlessly setting goals and crushing them. By 31 years of age, I had achieved a certain level of success which I thought would equate to happiness. I was wrong. I always felt a void, like something was missing, and I'd try to fill it with more success and achievements. I'd get home at 5pm on a Friday night and despite being able to do anything, go anywhere or buy anything; I had no desire to. It was in that moment that I realized that it was people that were missing from the equation. We are social creatures and I had been living like a lone wolf. With that breakthrough, I spent the next year investing my time and energy in people; I developed deep and mutually beneficial relationships, I spent more time with my family, I started a mastermind group to stay in touch with and be accountable to on a daily basis, and I started hosting networking events. As a result, not only am I happier and more fulfilled, but I've also found more success in every other area of my life.

I hope my 3 insights have been of value to you. If you have any questions or if I can be of service to you in any way, please send me an email at joelmartinmusic@hotmail.com. I'd love to hear from you!

Your friend and ally,

Joel Martin

Joel Martin

Joel Martin works at Metalworks which is one of the top entertainment companies in Canada, he's released 12 albums as a singer/songwriter, he's a judge for the Juno Awards, he runs some of the biggest events in the Greater Toronto Area, he's an investor in real estate and the stock market and he's also a professional poker player.

You can find out more at www.joelmartin.ca.

Humble Beginnings

~

By Dr. Joseph Radice

I grew up the son of an immigrant, coming to this country at 3 years of age. My parents come from a very small rural town in southern Italy where they grew up herding sheep and tending to crops. Having an agrarian background and with school not being a priority, or available, their education was poor to say the least, and as such, they were essentially illiterate. When they came to Canada, they didn't speak English and had no major skills to speak of, just the willingness to work hard and make a new life in this wonderful new country. It was a fresh start you might say. My father had a knack for working with his hands. He was certainly motivated to learn a trade, and eventually became a welder. He would be a blue collar worker his entire life. His wife of 58 years was, and still is, an excellent stay at home mom.

I think its important to point out that I was an "only child." You would think that this would give me the advantage of ensuring that I would have all of my parents undivided attention. That I would be spoiled. Well it didn't quite work out that way. My father was very strict. I had a specific set of chores to do on a daily basis. And if I didn't do them, my father would scold me. If they weren't done after being scolded, the punishment would be kicked up a notch to a spanking. Believe me when I tell you, I could tell when my father meant business. All he had to do was give me "the look" and stare me down. I learned at an early age to dare not question his authority. (A trait I have not been able to pass down to my children!)

It wasn't any different when it came to my education. My father told me on many occasions that he came to this country for one reason only. To provide me, his only son with a better life than he had. He did not want me to be a simple labourer. He knew the value of a good education. He often told me that he would make sure I would go to work with a briefcase in my hand, and not a shovel. So he placed a very high premium on a good education. He would be disappointed if I did not do well on a test. If I got a "C" grade he would immediately say, why didn't you get a "B"? As I worked harder and my marks improved to the "B range," he would say, "why didn't you get an A?" Essentially, what my father was doing, was raising the bar, and forcing me to improve on myself. I really wanted to please my parents, especially my father. So I would work harder and harder to make him proud.

In those days, parents wanted their kids to have mainstream jobs. A profession, a trade, or to go into a business. Children, especially those of immigrant parents, were not encouraged to follow there dreams. I remember my uncle asking me at the age of 7, what I wanted to be when I grew up. I told him that I loved staring at the moon and stars at night. I told him I wanted to be an astronaut, and one day go into space, and walk on the moon. Sounds pretty cool eh? Well rather than encouraging me to follow my dreams, he took out his hand and slapped me in the face. Then he said, "get a real job... become a lawyer!" I remember feeling inadequate and I was crushed! Although our parents and elders meant well, I realize now this approach did little to foster my self esteem.

I hope that I have now given you have a simple understanding of what I felt like growing up. I essentially felt like I was never good enough, and became addicted to the approval of my parents. These feelings of being inadequate spilled over into my everyday life and I believe, denied me the validation I so desperately craved from my peers. I believe that under these conditions, I didn't do what I wanted to do, but what I believe was expected of me. I dared not venture outside this circle of comfort for if I did, I may very well upset my sphere of influence and those whose approval I desperately seeked out.

When this happens, you are not a leader, but a follower. This is what happened to me. One becomes afraid to try new things and as a result you become stagnant in your growth. You develop a fear of moving forward proceeding in different directions. You become more concerned about what people think rather than developing and growing as a human being. You set the stage for sabotaging your own success!

This brings me to the heart of my topic. Although I may appear to be successful to most people, there are so many things I would do differently. The number one thing is to not be afraid. I would not be afraid to venture out, to speak my mind, to take risks. And most of all, I would not be afraid of what other people think. In my experience, this is the number one reason that people end up sabotaging their own success.

It took a long time for me to jettison my emotional baggage, and create the professional life I wanted. I wanted to be a leader in my field, cutting edge so to speak. Not just clinically but also in terms of practice management. I love dentistry, and am passionate about what I do. I am the only dentist I know that doesn't golf. I actually find doing root canal work much more relaxing and stimulating! How crazy is that? My hobbies have to do with learning as much as I can about everything that I do. I love taking continuing education courses, in person and on line, and have been called a "CE junkie" by my staff.

Because I love what I do so much, it does not feel like work to me. I made a decision to step outside my comfort zone and take risks that I would have not thought of doing years before, or at least when I was in dental school. I wanted to be the most modern and progressive dental office in my area. This turned out to be one the largest contributing factors to my success. I have surrounded myself with all of the latest toys and gadgets that modern technology has to offered. Remember that comfort zone I talked about earlier? Well listen to this.

When I graduated from dental schools, computers in the dental office were basically unheard of. They were unproven, expensive, required training and were nothing more than glorified databases. Well, I was one of the first to acquire a personal computer for my front desk, and later for every operatory in the office. My dental colleagues thought I was spending money needlessly, overdoing it. Needless to say, computers are used for everything to managing the patient files, scheduling, doing the office accounting and for education. Computerization is now essentially the mainstay of any office.

Other dental offices prided themselves on having a large selection of current magazines for the patient waiting rooms. Our office was one of them. I was one of the first to put TV's in every room of my office. This allowed me to provide my patients with information on a variety of dental topics and truly de-mystified many procedures that patients feared. Not to mention helping the time go by faster rather than sitting there worrying about there appointment. In office games and Wi-Fi soon followed.

Also in the early part of my career, I was one of the first to dive into computerized dentistry. I thought it was fascinating. This is where the dentist uses a computer, a CAD/CAM tool, to fabricate dental restorations, rather that take impressions and send it to a lab, which was the standard of care at the time. Using CAD/CAM was considered by many to be inefficient, expensive and provide lower quality dentistry. My colleagues thought I was insane. Our office now provides high quality, superior restorations in a single visit. This turned out to be a better investment than the Ferrari I wanted at the time. I haven't looked back. The same can be said for the laser I acquired for the office shortly there after. Not mainstream at the time, but now every office has one.

The take home message I want to leave you with is that you can achieve anything you want to as long as you are open minded and willing to step outside your comfort zone, to take the necessary actions to make it happen. Do not fear change, but embrace it. Do not be paralyzed by fear and inaction. Continuously educate yourself. Never stop learning. Don't be intimidated and afraid to surround yourself with people that are smarter than you are. Success can be thought of as merely learning from a series of failures. A wise man once said everyone wants to live on the top of the mountain, but all the happiness and growth occurs while you're climbing it. Remember that little kid who wanted to be an astronaut? Be brave. Don't reach for the moon, when you can reach for the stars.

Godspeed.

Dr. Joseph Radice

Award winning public speaker Kiro Shahata, is the founder and visionary of Inspire2dream, an organization which uses motivational speaking and crafted workshops tailored to inspire and develop future leaders. As a conscious and caring non-profit organization, Inspire2dream strives to awaken the inner lion, and guide it through the journey of knowledge and empowerment.

Come Out, Come Out, Wherever You Are!

~

By Karen Kessler

In a nutshell, I now live in the light of day.

In the before times it was all about me, so I perfected hiding.

It started when I was so excited to step out as an entrepreneur and coach. I ignored everything I didn't want to see. I was excited and pursued the hallucination that if I thought positively; everything would all work out perfectly.

Well it didn't. In fact, instead of making good use of all the smart decisions I made – like giving myself a $60k start up loan – I spent my time nailing my ostrich impersonation with my head planted firmly in the sand.

In truth, I set myself up for total failure. The start up loan was essential; the problem was that I did not seek guidance on how to use it. I assumed, incorrectly, that all my successes in my previous careers would easily carry me through into entrepreneurship.

I had the credentials and experience as a coach for more than a year now. I really didn't stop and think about the possibility that being an entrepreneur – a true CEO of my own company could be a skill gap.

They say its 'what you don't know, you don't know' that always gets you.

You will likely laugh, but I was truly shocked when business didn't just…happen. I had convinced myself so thoroughly that positivity was the key. I had funnelled every fear and concern into my positivity. Even though my failure happened slowly, finally accepting it was a tough blow for my ego.

The more I failed, the more I hid it from the world. I put on that tight smile and told everyone that things were fabulous. I worked harder and harder for it to be true. Long hours and soon the lines between me and my business; between my marriage and my business all blurred and disappeared.

The sand around my ears was curiously absent of ideas on how to turn things around.

Now follow this for a moment. If my head was in the sand, then what was sticking up? Right. As with most people with their head in the sand, it takes a very large kick in the pants to get their attention. For me it was the end of all credit options. When I finally could no longer pay my lease.

It was only when all independent options were exhausted, did I finally reach out.

I still shake my head at how simple things suddenly became. If only I had chosen to step up and ask for assistance at the beginning.

I learned a most valuable lesson. There are three choices for my focus, a) solely on me, b) solely on others, and c) a joint focus of self and others. A joint focus always means I flourish.

My behaviour demonstrates which focus I have. When I want to hide, I am making it all about me. When I choose to serve until exhaustion, then its all about others. When I choose who to serve and insist on being fully resourced in business, as a woman, and as a coach, then I know I am building sustainably.

Now its time to share with you HOW I go about having a sustainable focus that creates ongoing growth and resiliency in my world.

There are three key elements that must be acknowledged and developed on an ongoing basis.

- Skillful CEO: A role that evolves as your business does
- Master Coach: Master your expertise and commit to ongoing development of your mastery
- Fulfilled Woman: Weaving in your passion and purpose

<u>Skillful CEO</u>

The CEO hat is an ever-evolving hat for an entrepreneur. What is required for a start up is vastly different than what a business requires as it grows through six-figures, multi-six-figures and beyond.

There are several factors that make up a skillful CEO and the key ones are;

- Knowledge
- Experience
- Inner Programs

Knowledge: When you step out as the CEO of your own business, it is critical that you have the knowledge required for where you are in your business life. If you look back on when you first took the reins as an entrepreneur, remember how many decisions and actions there were.

Always have a mentor who you intend to grow beyond. If they continue to grow, then you may stay with them for a very long time.

Experience comes to us over time as we search out and apply the knowledge. The more experience we have at any level of CEO makes it easier for us to apply our knowledge to that level. The key is that every time we really master a level of business acumen…our business grows! That sounds like a good thing – and it is – be prepared to have huge gaps at this new level that you will need to fill.

Expect the discomfort and confusion that comes with the initial steps of learning. Without truly understanding what you are experiencing, you may decide you are failing…even though you are succeeding!

Inner Programs: Ever try to make a tool work for a different purpose than it was designed? Its clunky and no matter how committed you are to succeeding, sometimes it just doesn't work.

That's what happens when you become a CEO of your own entrepreneurship the first time.

You will attempt, out of your awareness to think, act, and make decisions the way they worked for you in the past. You will even try to motivate yourself the same way.

The gap is much larger than you think.

Think about your previous career. If you successfully paid your bills with that career over a period of time, then that will be your primary career programming. Your programming is all the things you do without even thinking about it. Your programming includes and certainly not limited to;

- Strategies
- Values
- Motivation

Strategies: Strategies are key programs that determine HOW you go about doing anything in your world. When there is a mismatch, or if key strategies are missing because you were never in an environment to develop them, then you will experience frustration and exhaustion in your world as an entrepreneur.

You have strategies for earning money, spending money, connecting with people, avoiding people, being seen, hiding, speaking your truth, being nice, making decisions, and many more.

Now, for me, I was missing key strategies that I needed to be a successful entrepreneur. I didn't know I was missing them. When something new came up, I reached into my tool belt of strategies and used the best match I had. Often it was like using a Phillips Screwdriver for a Robertson Screw (star for a square). I was always wondering why I wasn't having the same success here as I did in my previous career – heck I was a Rockstar there.

Some of the strategies that were inadequate for the job were

- Strategic Decision Making
- Wealth management
- Time management

Values: Your values determine what you spend your resources on outside of your awareness. They are deep in your unconscious and developed over time. They were influenced by your family, friends, culture, and your decisions about whether to accept or reject what was important to those closest to you.

You can say you want something in your world. But, if you have been working on it for longer than six weeks, then you just do not have the values programs to achieve it right now.

As a Master Results Coach, I know the secret to eliciting your most unconscious programs, like values, in mere moments. There is a treasure trove of information in your Values you can use to create success.

Motivation: People often wonder why they were so motivated in their last career but lose it when they jump to entrepreneurship. Or they are only motivated when things are financially desperate. You can choose as the CEO of your business to design your new workplace to create ongoing motivation, designed just for your programming once you know what it is.

Master Coach

If you are going to provide a service in the world – make it a good one! Make it a service that does as much for you to provide it as it does for the other person to receive it. This exchange of energy in the form of money for value is always a win-win.

Being a master is more than a title on your business card. There are many elements required for you to legitimately and ethically own the title of Master. Here is an example of how a Coach may own the title of Master.

- **Legitimacy.** Be backed by an organization that sets/exceeds international standards and ethics. Boards confer the right to use letters after your name that communicate your dedication to maintaining these standards and ethics

- Have a **Proven Process** to obtain results with your service every time

- Be so committed to your clients that you offer a **Guarantee**

- Have **Integrity**. Be very clear and focused about who your service is for. Only offer your service to people you know will benefit fully from your service

- Dedicate resources towards your **Continual Learning and Development** as a master in your field

- **Experience.** You have solved the same problem in your own world that you solve for others

- Resource continually with other Masters who are ahead of you to **Mentor** you on your journey

The Master Coach that is truly aligned with her service builds a business that fills her every day. She is committed to offering and delivering a service that shortens the path to solution for her clients. To provide a much shorter path than she travelled.

Fulfilled Woman

Entrepreneurship is not for everyone. The start up phase especially requires a great deal of time, money, and energy to create the momentum in the beginning. This will require a redistribution of resources from other areas of your life – family, self, health, etc.

Focus on self from the beginning is key to designing your business from the inside out. How will this business serve me? How will it fill my wallet and my soul?

There are three key tips for longevity as an female entrepreneur that I have learned from the fabulous women entrepreneurs I have had the pleasure working along side over the past six years. In fact, be sure to read my mentor Dr. Kim Redman's chapter in this book as well.

1. Serve in a way that lights up your **Passion.** Harness the need to make the past pain utterly worth it.

2. Choose to work in your **Feminine Energy** often. As a woman, your feminine energy gets more done with less energy. To do this, stay connected to why you are doing what you are doing.

3. **Community** is key. You are the average of the five people you spend the most time with. So, design your tribe to support you fully as an entrepreneur and as a woman who has many hats. You need people who will be there for you in the following ways;

- They will hold you accountable

- They will kick your butt when you hide

- They will hug you when you are frustrated

- They will only allow you to vent for 10 minutes (do a good job, time is ticking!)

- They will be the first to celebrate your achievements

- They will remind you of how amazing you are when you need it

- They know how to give and receive – win/win/win all the time

- They value learning and personal growth

- They know how to let their hair down and have an amazing time

Singular focus on any one of these three will create a lopsided and limping enterprise. All three must be woven in together. I plead with you to weave them all in from the beginning! If you have already begun, then start weaving now. Seek mentorship and update your programs to allow for your success. Then we can all stand in the light together.

Karen Kessler /// www.chooseresults.ca /// 705.294.4242

Karen Kessler

Celebrating her second international award for women in business in as many years, Karen Kessler is the Entrepreneur's Launch Expert – where results count. She is passionate about providing access to the skills, tools, and perspective required to build a passionate business; one that fills both your wallet and your soul. Karen understands the importance of mentorship, coaching, and following a model that works - it provides the shortest path to the service we are here to provide in the world. Karen is known for her leadership, integrity, and focus on results. Her reputation grew as she progressed rapidly through leadership positions in corporate, government and now the NLP Community as their lead Business mentor. ChooseRESULTS is narrowly focused on entrepreneurs launching or re-launching in the social entrepreneur space. They are ready to capture the skills for the highest human potential for self and other. The journey begins with the Designing Your Destiny™: Leadership & Empowerment Weekend; an experiential training that introduces what is so different and compelling about Dr. Kim Redman's Quantum NLP™ and how our community of Board Designated NLP Practitioners are leveraging their skills and designations to create international legacy here and now.

Quantum Leader™

~

By Dr. Kim Redman

Building a company from nothing into 7 figures and beyond, becoming one of a hand-full of elite Board Designated Master Trainers in both Hypnosis, and Neuro Linguistic Programming (NLP) globally, being the first woman in the history of our field to found a new board supported development in our industry, QuantumNLPTM aka QNLPTM, receiving my doctorate and simultaneously founding the international field of Quantum LeadershipTM....these are the usual things people want to speak with me about when enquiring about my success. While I am certainly proud of those accomplishments, they are the wrong things to ask me about if you are really serious about the HOW of it all when it comes to entrepreneurial success.

As impressive as that list might sound, those things are the WHAT IF, the after-the-fact of it all, the result of me following my WHY of it all, and struggling through the HOW of it all. Strategic thinking is a learned skill and it follows a pattern of Why-How-What- Results/

What Ifs. In that order. So if we are really speaking about success, we have to begin at the beginning...the Why of it.

The historical WHY of it all:

For me, the why of it all began when my ideal childhood turned into a teenaged nightmare. Becoming a teenager triggered a host of generational family dysfunction, daily chaos, and pain that included physical abuse. Just before my 18th birthday, I was strangled, went to the Light and came back. I needed to find out why something like that could happen to a loved, planned child like myself. I needed to find a way to change the generational family patterns and learn how to choose an empowered path, because an empowered path was the only way to stop the pain, for myself first, and then for others.

This put me on my Life Path, changed how I approached my life, and led me to study behavioural psychology, learning methodologies, Shamanism and Mysticism, emergency and integrated medicine, and quantum physics. I learned theatre skills and stage craft, toured professionally, founded a company that originally worked with at-risk youth, learned all about mindset, mentorship and coaching, and eventually turned the company into the empowerment vehicle it is now. Creatrix Transformational Solutions Inc.; Empowering Leaders to Empower Others.

A tragedy became one of my greatest gifts, opening me to the journey of growth, gratitude, love and the 'happy, healthy, wealthy' that go with a life of empowered service. When I started, there were very few women to model from. Now we seek to give those gifts to others, in a gentle and joy-full experience, rather than the 2 x 4 school of hard knocks that I followed. Welcome to my leadership and empowerment mission.

What I Learned in the Light...

Quantum Nugget #1

An Empowered Life Requires a Blueprint:

The difference between those who succeed and those who perpetually struggle are not their circumstances, or age, or gender. The difference is in HOW they think and WHAT actions they take based on how they are thinking. I needed to change how I thought about thinking. Verbs vs. nouns and adjectives. Actions and behaviours vs. a focus on emotions and analysis. Even love is a set of actions in ancient mysticism. Could you act lovingly towards a stranger? Of course! Thinking "it's all love" is a good start…next comes "lovingly doing".

I used to think about lots of actions, in my head of course, and was forever waiting for the perfect circumstance, or for the "right" time, or for someone's permission. Dying and coming back, taught me that all of those excuses are illusions. Truly, the only time we have IS now! Start now. Today.

What I learned that I use now; commitment is a set of actions!

Most of us start with lots of excuses. Especially the talented people. Talented people use their talent to hide their lack of skill. Harvard Business School did a recent study that showed that the more talented you are, the faster you fail, and this is especially true of women.

How do you really commit, using a set of actions rather than an idea? DECIDE to succeed first, no matter what obstacles are before you. It's an in-your-gut-no-matter-what type of thing. This means you decide to do the journey of continual learning and skill building. It's not always easy, but it is simple. Learn how to make a real commitment where you course correct along the way, rather than a conditional commitment based on how uncomfortable you are. As we always say, "Growth and comfort do not hang out at the bar drinking together." When the pain gets big enough, most of us will grow. How much pain we need in order to grow is within our control. Action faster.

Here are some examples:

Talented people say, "I don't know how to do __X__", and then they procrastinate.

Skilled people say, "Let me learn this faster!". Learning becomes an action item, with a date!

Talented people say, "When I have enough (time, money, energy, support etc.), then I will (start, change, stop, grow etc.)".

Skilled people begin building a reality, with an action plan, that is in writing (as opposed to just a mantra), and that has been reverse engineered. They often go to someone already successful and ask for an opinion on their plan. Doing it in your head equals poverty and failure. If this is you - change it!

For me this ability to decide on success, and action a commitment was realized through the process of obtaining two work visas, receiving landed immigrant status, and eventually receiving citizenship into Canada. This allowed me to build a life with my soulmate, husband, and business partner. Challenging? You bet! Worth it? It's priceless. The rewards usually are quite large because along the way you grow, and evolve, and growth is what most of us fight against.

Quantum Nugget #2

How to Decide:

One of the techniques I am asked about most often is how to make a quick decision from the host of possibilities that keep us spinning. Here is a fast technique, that I use often, and we teach it as part of the Quantum Leadership TM set in our Designing Your DestinyTM Leadership weekends:

1. Ask yourself if this action (X) will get you closer to your goal, or further from your goal.

2. If the answer is closer to your goal, then ask, "How can I _(X)_"

3. This will give you just a few key actions to choose from

What I wished I had learned faster:

Surrender to the process faster. Along the way, I needed to let go of ideology and beliefs that didn't suit me, release (entirely) the concept of being right, and look to my life as the evidence of whether or not I was on track. There are a couple of clear red-flag indicators that the shamans taught me, that most people ignore because of ego.

<u>Quantum Nugget #3</u>

Actioned Focus:

What are you more attached to? Happy, healthy, and wealthy…or being right? Most of us say happy, healthy and wealthy, and really mean that we want to be right. It's pretty easy to spot. Anywhere where there is drama (including with self) is an area where we are more attached to being right than we are to success. Our focus is in the wrong place.

Drama is the hands-down indicator that old, outdated programs are running, and we can't access our resources consciously. We often don't even know that we have a need, never mind being able to resource that need. We still need our unconscious need met. So, what do we do? We act out with drama (the drama queen, martyr, or the bully are some of our faves) and through our drama, we get our needs met. In coaching, we call this secondary gain. Our needs are valid. The HOW of it all is what needs to shift. When we speak to the recipe of success, being fully resourced as a human being is the most overlooked ingredient. It's hard to be resourced if you don't even know what you need!

Since our industry guarantees a change in behaviour within 30 days or less, focus is really important. Your behaviour tells you where your focus is. We ALL automatically action our focus, so paying attention to your behaviour becomes key data. Ego smash alert: Talk is cheap and deeds speak - so what you DO is the real indicator. We can all speak at a more evolved level than we can action at. Remember that growth is a journey, and as we say at Designing Your DestinyTM, "When you are done, you are dead, so let's just focus on the next step!". Course correct as soon as realize you are off track.

Quantum Nugget #4

How to Change Your Focus:

Step One: Pay attention to your self-talk. Is it success based, or excuse based? You can't stop a thought without many years of meditation, but you can change it. NLP Axiom: Our focus determines our behaviour. Our behaviour determines our success. Watch your behaviour. Is it the behaviour of excellence? If not, reach out to a mentor or trusted peer - fast! In our field, the reach out time is 72 hours!

Step Two: Pay attention to the level of drama around you and in you. Choose to spend your time, money, and energy on the things that you say are important. List your top three important areas, and note whether they get priority resources or leftover resources? This is what boundaries are about: choices and consequences. Make sure you are setting healthy boundaries. This is a skill we need to teach all clients, even our elite clients. Men are occasionally taught this at work, and usually do not bring this home. Women are socially taught to skip this altogether! Happy, healthy, and wealthy all require this skill.

Quantum Nugget #5

Healthy Boundary Recipe:

Step One: When you are asked to give your time, money or energy to any endeavour, always say "Thanks, let me get right back to you." This gives you the space to undergo the next steps.

Step Two: Decide if you really have it (as opposed to wanting to have it). Determine the opportunity-cost for giving this resource to this request. If you do not have it, say "I'm sorry I can't do that right now". If you do have the resource to give, go to the next step.

Step Three: Decide under what circumstances you are wiling to give this resource item of time, money, and/or energy. It is the person doing the favour who sets the conditions, not the person doing the asking! Also, decide the consequences (like not babysitting at all) if the conditions are not met.

One of my most quoted phrases is, "healthy boundaries create the safe space for change to take place". Go create those boundaries and spend your resources wisely!

In Conclusion:

The journey itself taught me the skills I didn't even know that I was missing. I learned to find the gap in my skill sets and to fill them quickly, both inside and outside of me. The harder gaps to identify are the ones inside of our own thinking and programming. Find a mentor or coach who can guide you.

We developed the Designing Your DestinyTM to give people some of the quantum templates for success. If you can't find a mentor, or are looking for resources, that might be an option.

Gratitude Gifts for You:

Send us an email to info@kimredmannlp.com, subject line: Quantum Learning, we will send you the 7 minute webinar on the 4 Stages of Learning and Inter-Dependence as a thank you for reading this chapter!

Mention this chapter and page number and receive a coupon of $225 to explore the Designing Your DestinyTM anywhere in North America.

www.creatrixdyd.com for dates and an overview of the weekend program!

Dr. Kim Redman

Dr. Kim Redman is the Visionary and Founder of Creatrix Transformational Solutions Inc. and the established international expert in the field of Quantum Leadership™. Kim is an empowerment specialist, and her creation of programs and synthesis of top quantum techniques is legendary. She board designates more graduates than any other combination of trainers in Canada. Some of her programs include the exclusive Go Quantum™ Leadership Program, where the candidates travel to exotic sacred sites and take part in ancient ceremonies of leadership; the Designing Your Destiny™ weekend program that completed a multi-city tour in 2014, and the Journey of Truth™ program that combines East and West skill sets for Quantum Success; a hands-on understanding of how to transform your life. This program is relaunching this year as a professional coaching program. Kim is also a published author and columnist. Kim's trains and mentors some of the top up and coming entrepreneurs and trainers in the country today and all of her graduates speak of her dynamic energy and training style that combines her diverse background of quantum physics, psychology, theatre, and shamanism.

Giving back and creating legacy are life concepts for Kim and she is an evaluator with the St. John Ambulance Therapy Dog Program. With her dog Apollo, she has earned the Priory Vote of Thanks from the Order of St. John for extraordinary volunteerism, as well as continuing to volunteer her time, energy and money to many other charities, and community initiatives. Kim's first ten years of service were focused on at-risk youth, and this led to her involvement in the award winning Chapter One Project that still runs in Buffalo, New York, today. This project, over 28 years of continuing studies in quantum science and energy, and her mission, have set the foundation for the work she carries on through Creatrix Transformational Solutions Inc.

Gratitude Gifts for You:

Send us an email to info@kimredmannlp.com, subject line: Quantum Learning, we will send you the 7 minute webinar on the 4 Stages of Learning and Inter-Dependence as a thank you for reading this chapter!

Mention this chapter and page number and receive a coupon of $225 to explore the Designing Your DestinyTM anywhere in North America.

www.creatrixdyd.com for dates and an overview of the weekend program!

If Today Was My Last Day

~

By Kirillos Shahata

If today were my last day, I'd want you to know that you are not alone.

You're not just 1 in 7 billion people populating this earth.

You have a reason.

You have a drive.

You have a purpose.

In a world surrounded by so many, I'd want you to know that your magnificent soul shines brightest through your character. I'd want you to know that you are perfect, just the way you are. Not because you don't have flaws, but because you embrace them. You leave marks, not scars. The presence that you share is felt just as strong as the presents that you give.

If today were my last day, I'd tell you not to lose hope. Despite what the news tells us, this world is still a loving place, humans are still compassionate, and we as humans still care wholeheartedly. And if I could have but one request, I implore you to push yourself to be all that you can be. Become your highest self. Don't be afraid to discover your purpose, and allow yourself to fulfill God's purpose for your life. Albert Einstein once said: "Life is like riding a bicycle. To keep your balance, you must keep moving." To me, nothing has proven to be more true. Life is absolutely like riding a bicycle. It's scary at first, tricky at best, but so rewarding once you get the hang of it. The key, as Einstein mentioned, is to keep moving. At the end of the day, the world won't stop because you do. It's up to you to make sure you keep moving with it. That's how you keep afloat.

The good thing is that over the past few years, floating has become my forte. Through trial, tribulation, and necessity, I grew resilient like a weed, thriving where others failed, and floating where I most definitely should have sunk. It's for that reason that I'm here with you. I want to share with you all that was shared with me, in order for you to enjoy the ride that we call life. And so, without further ado, I give you my top five pieces of advice to help you keep moving forward.

Play your hand. The fact is, life is random. You cannot choose the country you were born in, the family you were born into, or the situation you were born with. Your cards were loaded from the start with a destiny of a hand that we'll never fully understand, nor are we really able to change. Rather than cursing that which you were given, work with what you've got. As the first Indian Prime Minister and disciple of Mahatma Gandhi, Jawaharlal Nehru always said: "The hand that is dealt you represents determinism; the way you play it is free will." Choose to play your cards. Sweep the house.

Embrace the struggle. Whether it's between you and yourself, those around you, the elements, the circumstances, or anything in between. So long as there is discrepancy, there will always be struggle. The key here is not to get down between what is and what could be. Whether it's between who you are and who you want to be, where you are and where you want to be, or who you're with and who you'd rather be. There will always be a bit of a gap, but so long as you're constantly striving for the latter of them all, that place where you'd like to be, well, then you're on your way to getting there.

Find the right people. You will encounter all types of people. That's just a fact. There will be those who give off a positive energy, who lift you, encourage you, support you, and motivate you. These are the ones whose hearts are filled with joy, and souls filled with love. Find those people. As much as I'd love to say that all are like these, the truth of the matter is they are not. There are some brewed with hatred, jealousy and envy. They bring bad energy into your life, bringing sabotage to your success. Avoid those people. If for whatever reason you cannot, forgive them 'for they know not what they do' (Luke 23:34). Ignore their provocations and keep moving forward. That is the only way to beat them. "The hand that is dealt you represents determinism; the way you play it is free will." The beauty of it is that the right people will come into your life and stay. The wrong ones will teach you a lesson and leave. Be grateful for those people; they have taught you something you need to grow spiritually, physically and/or emotionally. At the end of the day, just remember that the goal is not to be better than anyone else, but simply better than who you were yesterday.

The secret to living is giving. The more you give, the more you get. That is one of the laws of the universe. Do not be afraid to give, even if you do not have much to give, you will be rewarded for all you do. Every bit helps. Give for the sake of giving. So many people these days give when the moment strikes, when the cameras are on, and when their generosity will be noticed. But true generosity doesn't come from boasting; rather, it's what you give when no one sees that matters the most. That will make the most impact, and that, in turn, will make you the happiest. This is brilliantly illustrated by a Chinese proverb: "If you want happiness for an hour take a nap. If you want happiness for a day, go fishing. If you want happiness for a year, inherit a fortune. If you want happiness for a lifetime, help somebody." True generosity makes you happier, healthier, and increases your ultimate life satisfaction. Give for others. It's as much as a gift for you as it is for them.

Forgive. Nearly everyone has been hurt by someone else. It's inevitable. As long as we keep interacting with each other, there will always be room for hurt. There are wounds that can leave you with permanent feelings of anger, resentment or even vengeance. Do not be blinded by resentment and anger. No matter how much you want to, do not seek revenge; it only proliferates the pain. Trust me, the only real way to get over anything is forgiveness. It does not mean that you forget the harm caused, but it means that you're bigger than it, you are more than it, and you are stronger than it. The first to apologize is never the weakest, but the bravest. The first to forgive is the happiest. Step up, be the bigger person, and watch yourself rise the moment you let go of the negativity.

Nowadays most people tend to neglect these vital components in our lives, and by doing so, they neglect their purpose. They forget that they were created for great things, and those great things begin with great people. So go on, step out into the world - forgive, play, love, give, and embrace your potential for greatness!

Because if today were my last day, I'd want you to know that the world needs more great people, and you, my friend, are just what this world needs.

Connecting with your inner hero is a choice that can be made at any time and in any circumstance. It is my strong belief that when enough of us choose to become our own heroes we can then become heroes for those in need, and together we can shift the consciousness of the world.

Kirillos Shahata

Award winning public speaker Kiro Shahata, is the founder and visionary of Inspire2dream, an organization which uses motivational speaking and crafted workshops tailored to inspire and develop future leaders. As a conscious and caring non-profit organization, Inspire2dream strives to awaken the inner lion, and guide it through the journey of knowledge and empowerment.

Proven Secrets To Success

~

By Laura Arci

Have you ever wondered how some people fast-track up the corporate ladder at a faster pace than others? Are you being overlooked for promotions? Are you interested in elevating your game and becoming a stronger better version of you? I encourage you to incorporate the proven game-changing ideas that I reveal in this chapter, into your daily routine. Ambitious, effective, confident, grateful, positive, genuine, dependable, committed, diligent, on-purpose and open-minded are many of the key characteristics and qualities that successful people possess. Consistent attention to changing your mindset and behaviour will empower you to develop many of these powerful character traits to take you to the next level. I am excited to share key instrumental Golden nuggets of wisdom and significant strategies that have attributed to my personal and professional success, despite the momentous challenges encountered along the way.

Effective delegation and time management need to be top priority focus items. Pay close attention to your daily schedule and staying on track. It is imperative that you delegate the tasks you are not good at or are not worthy of your full attention and invest your time in the highest producing areas where you will capitalize the most, whether financially, personally or in business. Most people spend most of their time doing tasks they are not best at and very little time on their best abilities. Think of your biggest time wasters and distractions. Put a plan in place to eliminate them from your life. Spend your time and effort controlling what you have power over. Allow what you cannot control to happen. Focus on high-priority thoughts, conversations and actions that yield the greatest results. Maintain discipline to stay on track and on time.

Create a life plan, which focuses on both business and personal goals. I have a simple 5-step plan that I follow; Think, Plan, Visualize, Act, Measure. Nothing wins more than superior preparation. Think about where you are today in your personal and business life, and project where you would like to be. What type of person do you want to be? What is important to you? What are your biggest distractions? How do you see your career evolving? What will make you happy? What type of people do you surround yourself with? What does your home environment feel and look like? What does your office look like? Do you feel productive in your work and home spaces? What are your qualifications? What do you need to progress? Are you an effective team player? Do you have job satisfaction? Are you satisfied with your remuneration? How do you feel about your appearance? Envision what changes you need to make to get to where you want to be. Focus on becoming a better version of you. Visualize and see the big picture. Have goals so big and awesome they make you excited to get out of bed in the morning. Establish goals that you want to achieve over the next two years in an aerial view and take the time to put a plan of action outlining the necessary smaller logical tasks that you must complete in order to achieve the much larger goals. Track your progress and celebrate each success, as you get closer to completing your goals. Visualization is imperative in helping you to realize your dreams. I strongly encourage you to visualize your success to enhance your experience, performance and behaviour. More importantly having a life plan will promote life balance. Your work is not your life. It is only a part of your life. We often get so busy getting from point A to point B and completing our tasks that we do not take the time to enjoy life and the journey of each task no matter what it is that we are doing. This is a huge focus for me because I can get caught up in being extremely busy that I must remind myself to slow down and enjoy the journey every step of the way.

A very strong work ethic and motivation to work diligently is paramount to achieving significant success. Anyone who tells you that they started their career and achieved executive status at a very young age while working very few hours is most likely not telling you the entire truth. You should strive to achieve a healthy work life balance, but it typically does not happen from day one. The first few years of my career at IBM, as well as my second career as a Real Estate Sales Representative, I worked effectively, efficiently and to be honest around the clock. These long hours and dedicated focus paid off for me. I utilized this initial investment of time and self-sacrifice as an opportunity to establish my identity, credibility and brand in organizations that hire highly talented individuals. My competition is always fierce. At IBM, I was extremely young for the job roles I held. Once I had established a solid reputation that I could swim and not sink no matter what scope of work was put in my lap I used that to my advantage to plot out a career plan. I engaged the expertise and support of senior executives and after 2 years, I was placed officially on the IBM VP Executive Fast path. My career skyrocketed and I had a very glamorous lifestyle flying around the world sharing ideas, conducting presentations, closing difficult multi-million dollar deals and making new connections and associations. After years of extensive sales and marketing experience, I have become a masterful sales negotiator and closer, which I leverage in my current role as a real estate sales representative.

Be authentic and genuine. Your integrity and reputation is critical to your success. Never try to be someone that you are not or that others expect you to be. Establish your credibility by demonstrating your commitment to achieving your goals, by being accountable, dependable, a solid team player and by your proven strong performance. What you say is what you will do. Never back down no matter how daunting the task. Always be up for a good challenge and continue to push yourself as long as it makes good business and personal sense. My entire life I have been pushed to my outer limits and each time I realize I can achieve more. Being a high performer others have always had very high expectations of the results I would deliver. This can put a lot of pressure on an individual if you do not harness your energy and apply it to your top priorities.

Talk less, listen more. Be a sponge and soak up information. Stay curious and be a great listener. Do not be a know it all. Possessing expertise and being confident is powerful but never think or act like you are better than others. Ideas are shaped when listening to other ideas. Make connections by taking one idea and connecting it to another. I recall vividly the first day I began working at IBM it was before my twenty first birthday. I was going to be a brilliant lawyer, but changed my career path when I was presented with the opportunity to work for IBM as a technical systems engineer. I believed that IBM was so fortunate to have someone with my caliber of skills. It was a humbling experience networking with a magnitude of extremely intelligent individuals daily. I quickly learned how important it was to surround myself with exceptional talent. I absorbed a great deal of important information by sharpening my listening skills, asking plenty of questions and by improving my social skills. Early in my career, before I would speak or make comments in a meeting I would ask myself does what I'm about to say in fact make sense? Many people make unnecessary comments or blurt out statements just for effect. What did they contribute to the conversation? Ensure that you add value and that your comments are on the mark with the conversation. As a real estate salesperson it is imperative that we ask a lot of questions to ensure we properly qualify our prospects and truly understand the needs of our clients.

Promote your personal brand so you can make the most of what you have to offer with your circle of influence and in the workplace. It is very important to effectively communicate, advertise and market yourself so that you are recognizable and differentiated as an individual in an authentic way. Surround yourself by a positive sphere of key influencers and inspirational people. Having a mentor is ideal and reading about great strategic leaders like Bill Gates, Steve Jobbs, Winston Churchill, Barack and Michelle Obama, Susan Wojcicki, Sheryl Sandberg, Dilma Rousseff, Richard Branson, Bill and Melinda Gates, Bill and Hilary Clinton, Warren Buffet, Oprah Winfrey, Nelson Mandela will teach you about what the very best do so you can emulate from those who have accomplished what some call the impossible. I emphasize the importance of the circle you keep close to you. When I began my career at IBM, I held diverse job roles from systems engineer, senior technical support, project manager, bilingual customer service, accounting, operations, direct marketing, catalogues and publications manager, marketing and sales. I gained valuable experience that gave me an overall aerial view of the business. I knew immediately as soon as I was in front of customers that I was born to be with people. No matter how complex the situation was I always had a great team collaborating with me to identify the challenges and put a resolution in place. The formula for business success is to find out what people really want, not what they say they want and give it to them. I had strong advocates who supported my every job move within the organization. It is very important to understand that if you are young, intelligent and you want to climb the ladder of success quickly you need allies. My first job opportunity from IBM US changed my life. My manager and several senior IBM Canada executives did not support this US job offer because they felt that there were other more senior candidates worthy of this role. My senior executive influencers stepped in to reinforce that the job opportunity was being offered to me and that I was more than deserving of the senior role and all the perks associated with it. I had just given birth to my first child Michael and after four months I was hopping on a plane to Chicago to meet my new team. The key to my success in moving up the executive ladder expeditiously was that I was constantly in the spotlight ensuring that the influential senior executives were well aware of my team's results, achievements and innovative competitive strategies that were successfully executed. I quickly established a reputation for achieving exceptional sales results, extreme employee loyalty, highly effective competitive assault strategies and leading edge marketing strategies contributing to high customer retention. Employees from around the world would request to be part of my team or transfer for short-term periods to spend time shadowing me. Currently, as a realtor, it is critical to the success of my business to continue to promote my brand and how I differentiate myself amongst other realtors based on experience, market knowledge and proven results. I have always been delighted to mentor and coach others as I bulldozed through my goals surmounting each obstacle I encountered in leaps and bounds. It is an exhilarating feeling to be respected and supported by your staff, peers, senior executive teams and especially your clients and key competitors.

Success is not solely based on achieving great business results. Make extraordinary opportunities happen. An abundance of love and great achievement involve courage, confidence, perseverance and taking great risks. It is a passion of mine to motivate and inspire others by sharing my journey and my proven secrets to success. It's never too late to make positive changes to your life. Take action and start now. As a young girl there were many negative issues and people that made me feel poorly about myself. My self-esteem was very low. I was made to feel like I was a loser who would never be good at anything. My life could have turned out very differently if I allowed toxic people and my daily challenges to control my life. Transforming yourself into the person that you want to be requires that you eliminate distractions, toxic people and time wasters, allowing you to focus on working diligently towards achieving your goals. When things get tough, backing down and giving up is never an option. You may need help to keep you motivated and inspired, but you must stay committed and keep moving forward toward your goals. Remember, life is short. Do what you love and be passionate about what you do. Remain focused and enjoy your journey.

Laura Arci

Laura Arci received full scholarship to attend the university of her choice and she graduated with Honours. She was the recipient of the distinguished Dean's Award with an impeccable grade point average ranking her in the top 10 amongst her fellow graduates. Laura received her Systems Engineer certification through IBM. She studied Harvard's Intense Business & Finance and Harvard's Intense Sales, Marketing and Social Media, sponsored by IBM. Also worth noting is her distinguished invitation to attend the Advanced Leadership, Executive Sales & Marketing Certification, hand-selected by IBM New York for 16 weeks hosted by Cash, Lehman & Associates and the Anthony Robbins team.

Laura began her career at IBM as a systems engineer. She speaks English, Italian and French and has held multiple bilingual roles. She was consistently ranked top 30 in sales worldwide and progressed rapidly to the ranks of senior executive holding roles in Canada, North America and Worldwide. Laura was ranked one of the youngest IBM executives with a continued proven performance and successful sales track record globally. As a visionary leader Laura was based in New York with direct reports worldwide and she was instrumental in leading IBM in the area of transformational change working significantly with CEOs and CFOs in the Fortune 100 sector.

Laura's visionary leadership and successful management of multiple organizations lead to the development of highly effective innovative Integrated Marketing & Sales Strategies, leveraging advertising, interactive web and e-Marketing, telesales, database analytics, direct marketing, social media, event planning and leading edge lead management and tracking systems. Her executive sponsorship and management of the IBM Xcellence publications and IBM Direct Server catalogues business proved to be very successful in driving increased sales and strengthening IBM business partnerships. Laura is a professional speaker ranging from speaking to a small group to an audience the size of 10,000+ business professionals. She has a magnitude of experience and continues to expand her knowledge by playing instrumental executive roles on multiple boards. Laura was pivotal in leading the IBM Global Marketing and Sales Review Board as the Chairperson with Senior Executive representatives. Laura was also a Board of Director at Blue Mountain. She has mentored 100s of people.

Laura is committed and driven to leading a positive, happy and healthy life. She is currently working on multiple writing projects focusing on self-empowerment and is focused on inspiring the lives of many by sharing stories of courage, confidence, perseverance and successful life-changing strategies.

Her passion for real estate consulting and investing has proven to be both lucrative and exciting. She has acquired and maintained a multitude of residential and commercial properties as part of her personal investment portfolio. Her first hand knowledge of the construction and renovation of properties has proven to be a great asset. She is a Re/Max Real Estate Sales Representative and has a passion for helping her clients achieve their goals. She enjoys working diligently representing the best interests of her clients exceeding expectation offering a proven total service sales marketing plan. Laura has established a tremendous network of contacts and clients, which she nurtures to promote her real estate referral business.

Kick Back

~

By Lize DelaRey Barkhuysen

Deep inside of me there was a little girl crying longingly to be loved and at that moment I felt the least lovable person in the world. I felt humiliated and ashamed and I didn't know how I was going to pick my life up from this lowest of all lows. I heard of people facing embarrassing encounters and being scarred but somehow my situation felt worse than others'. I mean, who has ever heard of someone turning their life around, after being admitted to a hospital three times for stress? I felt as if this stigma was stuck to me forever.

The lethal amounts of stress I constantly had to endure consumed all my rational thoughts and I almost lost my life because of it. An extreme, drastic and radical wake-up call forced me to face reality. Lying in ICU on my third hospital visit with a crushed left hand, left foot and my pelvis broken in five places forced me to look deeply and critically at the series of events and trauma that brought me to this point of no return. Each of the previous times I was in hospital my friends and family warned me to get out of the toxic marriage because the next time I might not get out alive. Their warnings were correct and true, but I couldn't get past my belief that I could and would fix my marriage, no matter what it cost! This time my family and Psychologist were adamant that I had to end this marriage for good. I knew beyond a shadow of a doubt that if I went back, like I did so many times before, I wouldn't have a fourth warning.

After a twenty-three-year marriage of verbal bullying I felt injured, unloved, abused, powerless and neglected. I understood my husband's childhood wounds better than anyone. Being adopted at two years old, he was shamed and disgraced in such a deep way that he never truly felt good about himself. Without my constant admiration, he felt like he was just a loser, a failure, zero; this realization hurt him profoundly.

I remembered how my husband regularly told me that I was stupid and silenced me, or his patronizing manner sent me fleeing to my room when he had visitors. One incident in particular stood out for me: he condemned my lack of general knowledge, and didn't count me worthy to escort him to his year-end function where he won a Porsche. In another incident he wanted to institutionalize me, projecting his fears on me.

Somehow believing I could fix him sucked me into his woundedness and his pain became mine. For years I allowed his belittling behaviour to paralyze me. I became a pitiful bundle of nerves with very little self-esteem, who lived to please him, thinking I was loving him to wholeness. When I realized that I meant more alive than dead I finally decided to get out of the threatening, unstable roller-coaster relationship of intense ups and downs. During this time I was confronted with my three biggest fears which played over and over in my mind: "Am I a failure because my marriage failed?" "Am I a failure because this is my third admittance to hospital?" "Am I mentally scarred, because I am using stress medication?"

The answers I finally came to were: "No, I am not a failure, although I tried valiantly but I could not help him, because I was not his saviour and not responsible for his decisions and actions." I believe that every person is inherently good, but we brought out the worst in each other. Once I took responsibility for my situation, my own healing, health and emotions I regained my long-lost self-confidence.

Today, I teach people about Emotional Intelligence. Now, each time I face my audience I am overcoming the fear of being unable to have a meaningful conversation. I speak to the outcasts at a Rehabilitation Centre on a weekly basis. When I speak to these addicts I see hope arising and I know that my example touches and changes lives. Lately, even the personnel sit in on my presentations desiring to be changed through the inspiration I impart because mine is not head knowledge, it was learnt through walking that dark road of self-forgiveness and realising my worth and value. The thank you messages I receive from ex-addicts have become my trophies of success.

I have addressed groups who have had abortions, endured sexual abuse as children, women who are used by pimps, people who are enslaved by gangs and are without hope and my messages offer them encouragement for a new beginning. I began small, but my presentation engagements are growing. Success begins by taking the first step. You don't have to be great to start, but you have to start to be great.

On my journey to wholeness I learnt three valuable lessons:

1) Self-management is essential.

2) Recognize your own skills and abilities.

3) Acquire the skills you don't have.

1) Self-management is about managing my fears, beliefs, positivity and especially my traumatic issues.

a) **Give up your issues:** Success begins with me. I had to manage my fears, doubts and insecurities. Someone told me, "Get over your issues, it is not about you." I had to let go of my ego, my own insecurities, my fears, doubts, failures and my past in order to be successful. My doubts brought me nothing but a feeling, it was time wasted that could have been spent on actions. When I decided to take action change began. Self-absorption had to be replaced by outer and other-awareness. When I was preoccupied with myself, I didn't believe in myself. I felt worthy when I do well. When I act right I feel right. To get there, I had to let go of my own insecurities and pay attention to other people. I light up with gratitude at the wonder of small insignificant things like when I can give my undivided attention and care to listening to others and seeing the thankfulness that someone cares. Nowadays I am more present instead of being trapped in the past, replaying stressful memories. Instead of seeking to impress or correct I now seek to make a difference and just to be authentic.

b) **Give up your Fears:** Fear paralyzed me, other-awareness freed me. I no longer feared failing to "please" others because I focused on giving to others. Whenever I fear, I immediately switch to focus on the other person. I decided it is better to live for this moment, in the now, as bold as a lion, than to cringe and be a coward simply because my fears limit my actions. Fearing to hear criticism when I acted was so debilitating! So I did nothing. When I did nothing I got nothing. When my circumstances could not worsen, there was nothing more to fear! I have already been rejected, criticized and humiliated. Now the fear of staying the same weighed more than the fear of change. Each action was better than doing nothing. I had no more excuses for not acting. I began to believe that I had the ability to make something of my life at least. Fearlessness allows you to constantly push yourself out of your comfort level to move in the direction of your fears in order to turn inabilities into abilities. Take courage: inch by inch, action by action, you can grow and expand.

c) **To believe in yourself you have to be faithful:** To do anything you have to believe in yourself, but faith has to do with faithfulness. You believe in yourself when you are faithful. Your internal conscience will confirm your faithfulness. In other words, if you wish to believe in yourself, and to have self-worth, you have to act faithfully in small things: Your yes must be yes and you must be honest. WHO you are is more important than your abilities. Character and integrity precedes self-worth. To have faith in myself I also have to trust that I will care for and protect myself: I must have boundaries. I reflect other people's faithfulness and values back to them: I can only trust those who are trustworthy. I only need to be transparent amongst those who I trust. People who can stick with me when the going gets tough are faithful.

d) **Create safety for yourself:** At times when I am feeling down or when I fall down and I feel I don't have what it takes in me, I don't put on a mask of indifference, pretending I am alright when inside the battle of my self-worth is waging. What I say to myself in such moments is paramount! My life doesn't come down to defining moments, each interaction, feeling and believe matters. I have to be willing to take the slaps, the criticism, the critical self-talk, I have to listen to it and approve of myself. I say, "I'm learning and progressing." I encourage myself that a baby step is better than no step at all. Mistakes are proof of trying. Actions quiet fears except with people who criticise whatever you do. Tell them to do it themselves.

e) We all need **challenge and comfort**, when I only received challenge without comfort I ended up in hospital. Now when I am challenged, I comfort myself. When I get overly comfortable I challenge myself. We choose how we create our lives. I use my will to dare myself to get out of my comfort and SAFETY zone. I never know what I can do unless I push myself and do it. Les Brown says, "It is easy to be on the bottom, it doesn't take any effort to be a loser. It doesn't take any motivation, any drive, any conquering to stay where you are on a low level but it calls on everything in you to change."

f) **Failure is a preparation for success.** When things are at their worst I remind myself that my passing through hell may be the preparation for my heaven. When I believed I deserved to be nothing and was worth nothing, I allowed verbal abuse! It gave me a chance to adjust my belief. When I got what I believed, I believed I was worth more.

g) There are moments when I can't believe in who I am now, then I believe in the person **I want to become.** That is my goal, my vision, and my drive. I often humbly admit that I need to sacrifice what I am for what I want to become! There is no humiliation in admitting that I am progressing. I am not a failure if I am learning.

2) Part of being emotionally intelligent is that you recognize your **own worth and abilities.** In order to stay on course to my goal of becoming the best me, I have to focus on what I love and am good at. Repeatedly I have to stop comparing myself to others and their abilities.

3) **Being skilled** at something allows you to feel confident. Skilful wisdom comes from being trained to do a specific task very well. We are trained by constant failure. To be skilled in your area of expertise means that you have to drill yourself over and over again until you master whatever you struggle with. Exercising my self-worth muscle meant I had to face many setbacks, and experience many obstacles. Facing challenges means you are still in training, the moment you permanently give up, is the moment you fail. Persevere in doing what is in accordance with your values and ideals. Be courageous and take pride in being the unique person that you are created to be.

Today I am a confident overcomer. It matters to me more what I believe about myself than what others think of me. I am no longer a victim of my past, I am an overcomer. My past has not defined, destroyed, deterred or defeated me, it has only strengthened me.

Lize DelaRey Barkhuysen

Lize is an author, speaker and consultant. Her goal is to help people achieve Emotional Intelligence which constitutes better relationships. Lize Barkhuysen has consulted more than 1,000 women and addressed thousands in talks throughout South Africa. As a speaker and seminar leader, Emotional Intelligence and Lize Barkhuysen are synonymous. Lize is the woman to study as she teaches you step-by-step how to go from emotionally wounded to wholeness in the quickest possible time. She believes change starts with WHO you are. She makes her case clearly and then proves it by her own remarkable life. She has researched for over twenty years in the fields of relationships, philosophy and psychology. Lize has produced written and video learning programs. She asks the question, "What if you really could transform your life overnight?" Lize's biggest credential is her personal story of going from a stress-victim to speaker. Lize wants to teach you to be the Hero of your own Story.

Excerpt from 'Memoirs of Michelle'

~

By Michelle Biggers

Dysfunctional family, exposure to violence, alcoholism, incest, rape, emotional and mental neglect and abuse, victim of violence to near death experience, drug addiction, multiple suicide attempts, apprehension of children by government, death of a child, ectopic pregnancies, miscarriages, abortions, multiple divorces and partners, prostitution, depression, institutionalization, clinically medicated, incarceration, eating disorders, family disintegration, homelessness, school drop-out, stroke and paralysis, loss of sight to temporary blindness, loss of hearing, electrical shock treatment, anguish, despair, brokenness, hopelessness.

We know we have challenges when these things are going on within our communities. But can you imagine if all of these traumas happened to one person? It took a full life's journey to learn how to heal and create an existence of love, intelligence, and peace. Everything that we encounter in life is a blessing. Now, some may argue that if there is a God, why is there so much strife, pain, and injustice in this world? I counter, that it is our own choices that create this sorrow. Oftentimes, circumstances dictate experiences we would rather not encounter, however, it is in the way we respond to those experiences that either make or break us. I was broken and made it through the other end. Most people, having experienced even a fraction of my past have not been fortunate enough to have made it. I am one of the lucky ones.

Between life-traumas and being a "productive member of society", I managed to amass and lose small fortunes and multiple properties. Taking a year to isolate from the corrupt and hypocritical social system that greed has created, I filled my mind with all the intelligence I could get my hands on. I devoured and read self-help books, covering everything from Existentialism and Redemption to The Power of Now, Think and grow Rich, The Road Less Travelled and much more. I bought any publication that might hold the answers as to why my life was so utterly destitute. I listened to self-help tapes, watched videos and lived, ate and breathed anything and everything that may provide an answer.

During this year sabbatical, I learned the three most important practices that not only healed my wounded soul but propelled me into greatness and oneness with the universe around me.

Becoming humble and beaten into accepting and loving myself was a turning point in my life, and a lesson well needed. Coming straight out of addiction, I weighed a mere 98 pounds at five foot six. I joined a local community group and found this was my first step to becoming whole. It is imperative for one's well-being, to feel as though we are a part of something greater than ourselves. Regardless of where that kindness and acceptance is found, for many, it is the one vital life-line. After thirty days clean, God again reminded me of my purpose. Driving home one day, I had an overwhelming sense of ecstasy and joy come over me. Inside my head and all around me, all I knew and felt was... the purpose for my being alive and well was to share my love and compassion with every other human being that had suffered through a journey as my own. I pulled over and sobbed with tears of happiness as I heard Him tell me that the only reason I was alive, is to love others. That's it. Just love.

Embracing service in every way I could find, I became valued again. I felt that there was hope, that I was not morally deficient, but that there was a solution to my isolation and anguish. As my social skills were honed, I became a leader within the fellowship and took on commitments for helping dozens of other sufferers, to hold their hand through the transition from hell to being ok. I sat on committees, held chair positions and made service to the community, my life. I followed His order.

There are few words that express the fulfillment of knowing that one has given hope and love to another. This was the first nugget of wisdom that sank in, finally.

Within this year of healing, I started to eat, not just survive on liquids. I nurtured my body with the cleanest and healthiest foods available. I gained thirty pounds and looked ten years younger as I developed a beautiful healthy weight and my skin became clear. I had energy and began to exercise regularly. I hired a personal trainer who subsequently became my partner. He groomed my new form into the most beautifully developed muscular body as I took on the physique of a twenty-year-old again. I went forward and won a Fitness award for "Absolutely Fabulous Women." This award is granted to women whom have had a positive impact on their community and beyond, through service and exemplary work that inspires others. Nutrition and exercise became my new addiction. I am grateful to this day, as I know I am honouring and caring for this God-given vessel that will see me through to a very old age, happily and with grace.

The third action or discipline that lead to my success was probably the most important, as, without it, nothing else gelled for me. I was a hard-core case and needed hard-core remedies in order to complete myself. Daily routine and ritual became a form of internal strength that is integral. There are many support and healing programs that are offered today from various self-help groups, doctors, institutions, community programs, fitness clubs, dieticians, ministers, and government. As much as these are all beneficial to some degree, there is a component which seems to be lacking in each of them. These solutions are not enough in and of their own. I searched for and made use of everything accessible. As a result of this, I created my own routine or program for life, and it changed not only me but hundreds of others while they either witnessed or became a part of this journey.

There is nothing finer than the solemn silence of Meditation. Every morning, before I fully awaken, I leave the house and go outside to sit on the ground. It does not matter if it is freezing cold with blizzard- like gales, or whether it is unbearably hot, I do it. I sit and close my eyes. I breath and clear my mind of all thought. If a concern enters my mind, I recognize it, allow it to be present for a second and then let it go. This process takes time when you first start practicing but with consistency and effort, the stillness will come easier and quicker. I listen to the sounds around me, the wind rustling through the leaves, the birds singing, sounds from far away, a neighbour's child laughing, and again, let thoughts flow into nothingness, as I slow my heart-rate and relish the love that envelops me. I begin prayers of gratitude and focus on how wonderful and joyous life is. I feel the breeze on my skin and am thankful to feel the touch of creation all around me. I sit in this trance-like state until my body shudders out a broken, stifled breathe, which tells me I am ok. Then, and only then, do I get up and go back into the house to awaken the children and start my day. On those rare occasions when I have not nurtured myself this way, my days have ended up in painful chaos, hurting not just myself, but the ones I love.

The most divine experience with meditation is the vision that is granted to me. One morning, while in stillness, I experienced what can only be described as an enrapturement. It is as if I saw the world through the eyes of the Creator, from the universe. I saw that I was to help other people by sharing my wisdom and wellness routine. I felt and heard that it was my duty to go public with my story and create a place of love and healing. It took me three days before I was grounded and able to talk about this vision of awakening.

I was not working, had no money, and was at the end of my years sabbatical, having depleted all funds remaining from the sale of my last property. Nonetheless, I knew that manifestation was already happening. I could FEEL it! Within six weeks of this vision, from nothing, I had purchased, renovated, and opened the doors of Whole Fitness Canada Inc. It is as if I sat back and watched all kinds of caring people come together and build this dream in front of my eyes. It was like watching an orchestra perform Beethoven's 5th. It was magical. I, to this day, take no credit in this miracle. I simply carry a sense of awe and gratitude at having witnessed it happen. Every day that I unlock that front door, a say a silent prayer of thanks for what I have been impossibly blessed with and know that it is not mine, but His.

Speaking with a dear friend some time later, I expressed how selfish I felt at having so much joy from seeing clients eyes come to life........ watching that "light" return to them. My friend pointed out that this is not selfishness, but to indeed revel in the pleasure of playing my role in the universe. That is my reward. There is nothing greater than knowing that as I allow myself to be a conduit of healing, it brings hope and health to my fellow beings. Words cannot express how humble it is to be honoured by being a part of another's journey mentally, physically, spiritually and emotionally. One of life's greatest discoveries is when we let go of ego, we are not our own. We become one.

Today, I continue to learn and crave knowledge and wisdom. Coming from a past of self-imposed strife, with hard-learned lessons and continually falling down, I have developed more courage and the power to get back up quicker and stronger each time. Now... I know how not to fall, but to only look forward and upward, as I learn how to fly.

There are many great nuggets of wisdom from beautiful souls that have had similar experiences. The best of myself that I can share with another is embracing them into a loving and supportive relationship, offer community engagement and hope for the acceptance of "oneness." To teach one how to still the mind and hear the heart. To heal the physical or broken body with healthy choices and exercise that honours the incredible self-healing machine we call our body. I am nothing less than grateful for having been blessed with all of the past, pain, and suffering included. It is only through this that I have become polished, been sculpted into the loving woman that God has created me to be. I live only for His will and higher purpose. I ask every morning.... "What do you want me to do today? Take me, I am Yours. Show me what I need to do". And every day His answer is the same... love others. That's it. Just love.

Michelle Biggers

Michelle Biggers U.E., Pastor, CEO, PT, WFCC

From a very young age, Michelle Biggers has been blessed with the gifts of vision and healing. At the age of seven, she experienced her first "spiritual" awakening and knew that there was only one purpose for her life, to help others.

Excerpt from 'Memoirs of Michelle'

Michelle has been an entrepreneur from an early age. She started teaching at the age of seventeen and opened a Private School of the Arts at age twenty-one. Throughout her journey of giving birth to seven children, three divorces, mental health issues, drug addiction recovery and overcoming other great challenges, she has inspired and lead others to come through their own journey as well.

Michelle went into marketing and advertising for some years and then left the business to take a year's sabbatical to re-open a unique Fitness Facility, Whole Fitness Canada, that trains the body mind and soul.

With two of her children still at home, she is the perfect example of how a woman finds balance in her life for running a business, working a fitness routine and running her household as a single mother. She can deadlift 185lbs!

Her days begin with prayer, meditation, and an intense workout. Michelle has maintained the physique of a twenty-year-old even though she is well over forty and leads a very busy lifestyle! Michelle is a "Absolutely Fabulous Women" Fitness Award winner, Certified Minister and recently, licensed Ordained Pastor. Michelle Biggers is truly a woman of strength, faith, and courage.

The Hero Within

~

By Parmida Barez

I spent most of my 19th year of life bed ridden, indoors or in the hospital. I had severe anxiety disorder, panic attacks, depression, and agoraphobia. It was a version of me that wouldn't be able to give talks and conduct seminars in front of hundreds of people as I do now. A version of me that wouldn't have the drive or passion to follow her lifelong dream of becoming an author and influencer in the field of personal empowerment. At the time I had lost sight of the "bigger picture" by allowing the noise of the outside world, and the noise inside of my head, to distract me from hearing the voice of my true calling.

I can now proudly say that those days are far behind me. What has remained as a reminder however are the important lessons and tools I have extracted from that period of my life; lessons that continue to shape me throughout my journey. I now recognize that within the depths of me, and within all of us there is a hero, one who silently holds our hand, awaiting to befriend us. When we turn inwardly to it, we begin to foster a special, life altering relationship with ourselves. Ironically, it is in our darkest hours that we sometimes find our brightest light, and if we so chose, we can rise again with a vigour, a passion, and a purpose far greater than we ever knew before.

Each of you reading this has faced, and will face obstacles and adversities in your own lives. Within these adversities there will be defining moments. Your actions during these defining moments will become the distinguishing factors between a life lived to your fullest potential, or a life left reflecting on "what could have been." Many years ago I made my choice. I decided that I was not going to settle for a subpar version of my life. Somewhere inside of me I knew that I had a purpose far greater than the condition I was facing.

Taking back my personal power meant letting go of the excuses I was telling myself, pushing past my fears, and no longer relying on other people as a crutch. It meant moving forward, despite the odds and uncertainties. On the journey to becoming my own hero, I have gained much and lost much. What I have lost, are many of my fears, anxieties, negative thought patterns and behaviours, as well as much of my self-inflicted unhappiness, helplessness, and victimization. In agreeing to become my own hero I have made a pact with myself to continually strive to become more self-aware, self-motivated, and compassionate towards myself and others. I have agreed to be more socially responsible, purposeful, and most importantly, to stay a life-long student.

Connecting with your inner hero is a choice that can be made at any time and in any circumstance. It is my strong belief that when enough of us choose to become our own heroes we can then become heroes for those in need, and together we can shift the consciousness of the world.

Here are three ways you can begin that journey today.

1) REFLECT

With a list consisting of work responsibilities, family life, health initiatives, hobbies, social activities, as well as successes and failures, life can seem like one big whirlpool of events. It is no wonder then, that we may not leave much space for meaningful solitude and introspection. Herein lies the problem. Living in a world full of distractions makes it easy to fall prey to habits, ways of thinking, and environments that may not be aligned with our true aspirations and highest selves. If you don't have evaluation measures in place, losing your purpose and direction in life can be easier than you think. The former is one of the reasons why it is of such great importance to MAKE the time, intermittently, to ask the important questions, de-clutter your mind, and re-focus your intentions.

What are my true passions? What are the causes I care about? Is the way I'm living my life currently aligned with my core values? What are some of my limiting beliefs? What environments am I exposing myself to? Are the people, places & things I surround myself with a help or hindrance to my emotional, mental and physical well-being? Do I over identify with my ego? Am I living a life that is truly meaningful to me?

Believe it or not, a lot of us may actually be afraid to be alone with our thoughts and feelings. To actively choose to look for answers deep inside our minds and hearts requires an openness, readiness, and frankly, some courage! We each have our own personal resistance to what we will find if we open up those gates to self. For instance, what past hurts will come up? What memories will we have to face? What if the life we are living is not the life we want for ourselves afterall? What if we have to own up to the hurt we may have caused others, or the hurt others have caused for us? And even if we are open to delving into ourselves further, we may not have the appropriate methods, tools or strategies to do so effectively. So, often times, we shut the door, lock it, and immerse ourselves in our technology, friends, work, responsibilities, social activities or even harmful substances that keep us distracted.

In each of our lives there are moments where we will feel uncertain, lost, confused, unsure, complacent or even get a sense that who we are at the time does not match up with who we truly want to become. If we don't take the time to "check in" with ourselves every so often, we may very well find ourselves getting stuck in certain places and phases far past their expiry. Ultimately this may lead to us missing out on our full potential and many of life's great opportunities. Being honest with ourselves, understanding our own strengths and weaknesses, and taking responsibility for our lives, puts us in an empowering position to create the life we truly desire.

2) TAKE ACTION

Finding a balance between self-reflection and action is also very important. Too much or too little of either can disrupt your personal ecosystem. On the one hand, spending too much time thinking, wondering and questioning, without taking the steps and actions necessary to implement the necessary changes, will keep you at a standstill. On the other hand, a stream of unexamined, scampered, inconsistent or mindlessly habitual actions will most likely lead you to a life without true fulfillment and direction. What is of importance, is to act with intention.

From personal experience I have found one of the best ways to cure fear or anxiety is to take action! One of the keys that have successfully helped me overcome my past phobias and conditions, has been to allow those fears and anxieties to propel me into positive action rather than immobilize me. Through experience and practice, much of your doubts, fears and uncertainties are eventually addressed and answered.

When I decided that I wanted to be a public speaker, for example, I used every chance I could get to do so. I dove head first into competitive speaking on top of that! I gained confidence through exposure and repetitive intentional action. Slowly most of the unknowns became familiarities instead. You can go at your own pace, but remember there is no losing when you're learning! Don't be afraid to be the first to volunteer, to try something new, and to push past your boundaries in a healthy way. Realize that some things will feel uncomfortable, that things won't always turn out as planned, but by stepping up to the plate and giving your best, you are strengthening your resolve, your self-reliance, and your belief in yourself.

3) STAY INSPIRED

So, how do we keep ourselves inspired to live our most purposeful lives? How do we keep ourselves motivated to both reflect and take action? I often say that motivation, or inspiration is a daily ritual, because it can easily slip right through your fingers if you're not careful! Some of the tools to keep me inspired to live my best life are as follows.

Visual reminders: I am a big fan of cultivating an environment that keeps me focused, inspired & grateful. I value the use of white boards, vision boards where I can write or draw my ideas; this is a great way to be reminded of my aspirations and words of wisdom throughout the day. Another tactic I use is intentionally placing trinkets or certain memorabilia throughout my home or work environment. These objects are special reminders of meaningful experiences I've had, my purpose, and my goals.

Inspiring Books & Media: One of the tools I find useful to keep me inspired is to read books, watch videos, listen to music & engage with social media accounts that are either positive, thought-provoking or growth oriented. There are also a few go-to sources that I can always count on to give me the boost I need. Waking up in the morning, sometimes I'll watch a short, inspiring clip to get me ready for the day.

Or throughout the day I might take out a pocket book of inspiring quotes. There are many ways to expose yourself to inspirational sources. The key is to make a habit out of not going too extended a period of time without infusing one of these inspirational sources in your routine.

Support system: The right support systems can be an imperative driving force in your life. Some of which include friends, family members, support groups, clubs, therapeutic council. It's always okay to ask for help or guidance. Although ultimately in life no one can walk our path for us, having an honest, well-intentioned, growth-oriented circle of friends or avenues of support can make all the difference on your journey!

Community Service: It's easy to lose ourselves in our own problems, responsibilities, ambitions. Volunteering, and giving back to the community with your time or energy not only feels good, but also creates a shift of perspective. It helps you see the bigger picture, and the role you play in it. It is also a great reminder that, no matter who you are, or what your circumstance, you can help foster positive change in the world, any moment you choose.

Parmida Barez

"Author, Award winning Public Speaker, Songwriter, Teacher and Philanthropist. Parmida strives to empower others to become the leaders, movers and shakers of their own lives. Both the breadth and depth of her experiences have equipped her with many life-changing tools, techniques and perspectives that she has dedicated her life to sharing with others on her journey."

www.parmidabarez.com

Our True Purpose

~

By Pat Di Rauso

Life is a blessing and what we make of it uncovers our true purpose on earth... Imagine awaking everyday to routinely catch an 8:00AM train for work and the consequences you would face if you should miss it...Now imagine awaking everyday and having the ability to catch whichever train you want at whatever time because you work for yourself and set your own schedule...

I am sure the latter entices you more. It certainly does for me! To awake to see another day in general is the biggest PRIVILEGE of Life but sit back and think how great of a privilege it is for you to awake on your own time...

Back when I first started in entrepreneurship, I did not think about the PRIVILEGE of having the ability to make my own schedule on MY time. All I cared about was making my business successful. Over time,

I realized that my biggest PRIVILEGE of all was achieving Success in Life. I view my success as a PRIVILEGE because I know that nothing is guaranteed. Seeing my success as a PRIVILEGE keeps me humbled and grounded. I graciously thank you in advance for allowing me to share my trials and tribulations with you and hope they bring solace and guidance to your own journey of success.

How many times does the following thought cross your mind,

"Is this where I am suppose to be today?"

and you reflect on it but uncertain what your answer should be. The mere fact that that thought crosses your mind is because you probably care about the path you choose to walk in life. In my earlier stages of life, nothing weighed heavily more than that thought. Through experiences though, I have been able to answer this question with more certainty. So… "YES, I am supposed to be where I am today!"

As the CEO of a music education franchise system, Arcadia Academy of Music, I have the great PRIVILEGE of educating the young minds of the future leaders of tomorrow through the art of music. I keep reflecting on the word "PRIVILEGE" because it keeps everything I do and say in perspective. This brings me to my first of a few nuggets of wisdom I would like to share with you:

"Treat life and all it has give to you as a PRIVILEGE" – All that you do, say and achieve would mean more to you and nothing would be taken for granted. This creates a healthier mindset and gives you the fight necessary to overcome any challenges you are faced with.

A 7-year old boy from Rome, Italy migrating to Canada with his family who had a good life there to make a better one somewhere else was unheard of back in 1972. But that was the character of my father, Carmine Di Rauso; an ambitious man that always searched for better. That kind of AMBITION was instilled in me from a young age and I continue to hold on to it to this very day as one of key elements to my success. At 11 years old, I entered the world of entrepreneurship selling peanuts at the old Exhibition Stadium in Toronto. As small of a job as it may seem, I took pride in what I did and through that experience I discovered one of my passions, which was interacting with people and more importantly selling to them!

I would soon come across my passion for soccer not too long after and had the opportunity to pursue it at a high level but as fulfilling of a career as that could have been, I realized that helping people meant more to me. This brings me to my second nugget:

> "Care for people like you would want them to care for you. Help people like you would want to be helped in times of need." – Compassion and the willingness to help others strengthen your character and bring out the best in you and in others you meet and surround yourself with.

As I was about to embark on the journey of becoming a police officer in 1984, my father asked me to come work with him at a music school that he was about to open in Woodbridge, Ontario. This music school would be called as it is known today as Arcadia Academy of Music and my involvement with it forever changed my life. This path I chose brought me great success and many a failures. Today I wear my scars of failures as my badges of success and growth. Failure was necessary for me to grow. Hence my next nugget of wisdom:

> "Failure is necessary to grow." – Failing is not a bad experience. To me, it means the effort you made did not fulfill your full potential. How you choose to react and learn from any failure will determine if you grow and fulfill that true potential at the task at hand.

In 1989, I married my beautiful wife, Loreta Di Rauso and made a decision to leave Arcadia Academy of Music due to personal strife with my father. I bought into a HVAC franchise system not knowing much about HVAC but felt confident enough to sell it! By 1992, I had my first son, Carmine Di Rauso and it was that year despite gaining a family, I almost lost everything else. In 1993, I had to start all over again and begrudgingly returned to Arcadia Academy of Music. I had no choice. No time to feel sorry for myself. I had a wife and son to provide and care for. Through that failure, I learned that the "grass isn't always greener on the other side" and when the going gets tough don't get going! Running from any issue is not the answer. Over time, I mended the relationship with my father and learned how important family is to your growth and success.

> *"Family makes the road to success easier." – Along the way, you are more than likely to encounter obstacles. Family becomes your rock; your comfort in hard times. Having a supportive family puts you in a better state of mind to overcome the obstacles ahead. They are able to remind you why you chose to take this path and what you are working towards.*

My wife Loreta, no matter how hard the times get, continues to show me unconditional love; show me what it means to be the best version of a partner in a marriage and brings out the best in me. She is my rock and I could not choose a better partner to spend the rest of my life with. My success today is owed a lot to her. Find your "Loreta". With a partner like her by your side, no goal is unattainable. By 1995, I had my second son, Francesco Di Rauso and Arcadia Academy of Music continued to enrich the Woodbridge community. My younger brother, Maurizio Di Rauso and I had a bigger vision that saw the expansion of Arcadia Academy of Music into a franchise system. In 2002, our father sold the company to us. One would think after my 18 years of investment, he would pass it on to me. But Carmine wanted to teach my brother and I a lesson which I have turned into my next nugget of wisdom:

> *"Never accept hand-me-downs. Work hard and earn the rewards… you will have a deeper satisfaction and appreciation for your success."*

As tough as that was to swallow at that time, today I cannot thank my father enough for teaching my brother and I that lesson. Because of it, the fruits of our labour stand tall today across communities of Ontario. With 10 Arcadia franchise locations across Ontario, the growth of the Arcadia brand through our vision has been a milestone throughout my journey to success. But gaining this success brought new challenges.

"With great success comes even more challenges and responsibility".

Cliché statement but so much truth to it. The more I succeeded, the more challenges I faced. I garnered more responsibility over many areas that resulted from my success that I did not have before. In addition, I had set even larger goals than the ones before putting more pressure on me to achieve them. With all of that, it was easy to get caught up in it and neglect the things that mattered to you like family. One of my biggest challenges has been finding a balance between family and business. It is tough especially when your whole family works with you as is in my situation. Sometimes it gets confusing distinguishing relationships: my son as my son vs. my son as a manager or my wife as my wife vs. my wife as the franchise administrator. It is a blessing to be able to see my family everyday inside and outside the house but when things get tough at work it becomes a challenge on how to approach them. Ergo, ensuring our family dynamics are not thrown off, we made a pact that we would leave all work at the front door of our home at the end of every day.

Building the Arcadia brand requires a team and the further it grows, the bigger the team required to manage it and the more protective of I become of it. If there was a disorder called "Micromanagement Disorder", I am pretty certain I would be clinically diagnosed with such. That was my next challenge. I battled with the fear that by letting go some of my responsibilities and entrusting other people to do it, it would not be executed to my standards and jeopardize all that I have worked for. Dramatic, I know but after 30 years of personal sacrifice and investment, there is some plausibility to this feeling. Think about if you just had a baby, and having to leave he or she with total strangers that you just met to help grow and nurture while you focus on other areas to provide for that baby. As daunting of thought that is, that is more or less what people with their own businesses do on a daily basis. That is what I do. I have gotten better at dealing with it. This is how:

> *"Find people that have the same passion, values and principles as yourself. Believe in them. Treat them the way you would want to be treated and make them your family."*

Over time, I realized that by bringing together the team around me and making them my family manifested a common belief in what we are all striving for under the Arcadia brand. That was enough to help me overcome my fear and without my current team today, the brand's success might not have been this fruitful.

As I wrote my chapter of this DYNAMO diary with hope that what I have to share inspires you, I reflected on three areas of my life that keep me going today which will be my final three nuggets of wisdom to you:

1. **Happiness, Love & Gratitude** – Find happiness within yourself, love yourself for who you are and be grateful for all the PRIVILEGES you have been given. Do not seek it in the materials you desire. Once you do that for yourself, share it with everyone else around you at its highest capacity.

2. **Love what you do! Believe what you are doing still has a purpose!** – Despite all my challenges I encountered throughout my journey to success, I would go through it all over again because simply put, I LOVE WHAT I DO! Loving what you do and believing in it brings solace in times of trouble and provide you the resilience and determination needed for success.

3. **Pay it forward!** Be a philanthropist! – Achieving success should be shared with others with hope they would be inspired to achieve

their own success. Use your established platform to give back to communities and inspire others!

I am a visual kind of guy and despite sharing my experience through my words, I wanted to chart out elements that aided to my success that you should try out in your life. Let's call the chart below the "Chart to Achieving Success" – according Pat Di Rauso.

"Who I am today is the person I worked on yesterday to make better for tomorrow!"

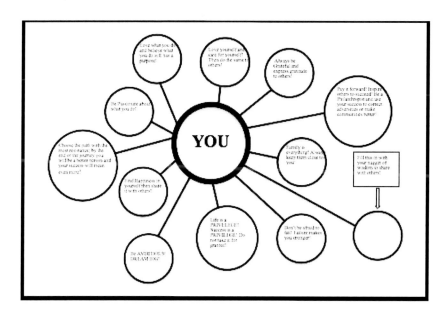

The future ahead of me will involve Arcadia Academy of Music. Arcadia has and will always be dear to me... Our family emblem! It stands for sacrifice, opportunity, honesty, commitment, trust and strength! I have grown with it in so many ways and we will continue to grow under the same principles adding even more academies across Canada and the USA. I know I will never retire but I will stand back and enjoy our success and enjoy life with my wife. Our next generation will continue our growth the same way my brother and I continued our father's dreams and I have all the faith that our children will succeed! To conclude, I leave you with this quote by my father and hope it makes a profound impact on you, as it did with me: "The only thing we have as people is our word. If we lose that, we have nothing left." – Carmine Di Rauso

Pat Di Rauso

Pat Di Rauso, born in Rome, Italy and raised in Canada is an entrepreneur and the CEO of Arcadia Music Group responsible for the Arcadia Academy of Music franchises across Ontario, Canada. Arcadia Academy of Music's concept is simple yet effective – providing a personalized approach to delivering music education programs through quality and vision. They believe that every child should be given the opportunity to be exposed to music, enriching their lives inside and outside the classroom and delivering music programs that revolutionize the way music is taught and learned.

Pat's passion for educating kids goes beyond the walls of music classrooms and into the soccer field as he volunteers at the Vaughan Soccer Club as their Executive Vice-President. Anyone that crosses paths with Pat notices how much of a passionate, charismatic, energetic and happy individual he is and he enjoys interacting with people. Being a community-minded individual, he is always involved in some sort of philanthropy and looking for ways to improve and empower his community. In his downtime, he enjoys spending time with his beautiful wife Loreta, and being a dad to his two sons Carmine and Francesco Di Rauso.

Harnessing Your Inner Leader

~

By Rick Denley

Leadership, much like life itself, is a combination of passions, purpose, and pursuits. People require leadership in many aspects of their personal and business lives. What I have discovered through my life and business challenges is that the same leadership qualities exist in all areas of life. Leadership is about guiding and inspiring people through life's personal and professional challenges, to be the best they can be and achieve goals they never thought possible.

In this chapter, I will share three leadership qualities that will help ensure that you are the best, most influential leader you can be.

Leadership Quality #1: Empower and Influence Others

Empowering means that you share some of your authority and responsibility with team members. You are giving your organization and team members a greater feeling of involvement in the desired outcomes. By giving team members greater scope and responsibilities, you are grooming the next generation of confident leaders. It may mean some extra mentoring for you at the start of the process, but the ultimate result will be more time to work "on" your business instead of "in" your business, increasing your ability to be a more productive leader.

In 2008-2009, during one of the worst economic downturns in the manufacturing sector in recent history, I took on a role leading a small systems integration firm. Understanding the organization had some talented individuals, I took the approach of elevating their responsibilities, instead of limiting them. Empowering them with specific divisional leadership responsibilities, tightly tied to the newly developed company strategy greatly reduced any pushback to the plan. It demonstrated to the staff that all individuals were respected and supported in their capabilities. These newly appointed 'leaders', like most, embraced the opportunity and accepted leadership with ease and enthusiasm. They led meetings, created assignments, and adjusted the strategy as they executed it. They collaborated well amongst their team members with my guidance via mutually agreed upon objectives and timelines, and began developing and further enhancing their own leadership styles and skill sets.

When you empower others, you are in effect leading from behind. You have positively influenced others to take on leadership roles.

"True leaders don't create followers, they create more leaders" Ziad K. Abdelnour

Leadership Quality #2: Be Your Authentic Self

In leadership, we are passionately inspiring and empowering individuals. The key is to harness your strengths to lead in a manner that is yours, not someone else's idea or style of leadership.

An interesting study by Deloitte University found that more than half of the leaders studied cover up some aspect of their identity when at work. It also suggests that suppressing your natural behaviour is linked with health issues including a decrease in immune system functioning.

Several years into my career in sales leadership, I sought the guidance of a partner in a placement agency, who happened to be my brother-in-law. He recommended I have a conversation with his business partner who specializes in executive search. I agreed, understanding feedback from an experienced recruiter would benefit me. We met and engaged in very productive discussions about my abilities, past successes, failures and what I was searching for in my career moving forward. I met my brother-in-law shortly after for debrief. What he shared with me was extremely interesting, and a little shocking. Having the advantage of knowing me on a personal level, through years of family related events, golf outings and in other social settings, he had the vantage point to compare this to my professional persona. What he observed was that my personality changed when in a business setting. This wasn't necessarily a bad thing, as he acknowledged my ability to convey confidence in my business and leadership acumen. This included a very polished professional demeanour that brings instant business credibility and strength of character. However, what he recommended that was lacking was what made me who I am. I enquired as to what this was? He said, in a word, likeable. He shared that my personality, natural body language and sense of humour, amongst other things, made people feel at ease and enjoy being around me. These were innate attributes that not everyone possesses and can be very effective in leadership. He reinforced the need for me to tie together my natural talents, including my story-telling ability, for example, with my compassionate nature with others. He looked at me, with a slight smile, and said "Just be you." So who exactly are you? To discover who you are as a leader, trust your natural instincts and the credibility of your past successes that have brought you to where you are today.

The Harvard Business Review published research by author and psychologist Daniel Goleman (well known for his documented theories on the importance of emotional intelligence in leadership) that uncovered six different leadership styles. He argues these styles listed below spring from different components of emotional intelligence:

1. Commanding: Leaders demand immediate compliance.
2. Visionary: Leaders mobilize people toward a vision.
3. Affiliative: Leaders create emotional bonds and harmony.
4. Democratic: Leaders build consensus through participation.
5. Pacesetting: Leaders expect excellence and self-direction.
6. Coaching: Leaders develop people for the future.

Think of those that have inspired you, those that you admire for their leadership abilities. Where do they fit within these leadership styles? Which dominant leadership styles would best portray Fortune Magazine's 50 Most influential Leaders?

Leaders such as musical superstar and lead singer of U2, Bono, whose tireless efforts to influence governments and companies to support his efforts in AIDS relief and raising funds to combat poverty and preventable diseases. Spiritual leader Dali Lama, who has spent over 50 years campaigning for peace, nonviolence, democracy and reconciliation amongst world religions. Actress and humanitarian Angelina Jolie, who joined forces with the UN's refugee agency in 2001 as a goodwill ambassador and as a special envoy participating in over 50 field missions all over the world including Iraq, Syria and Pakistan in efforts to end a plague of rape in war-torn regions. The CEO of Starbucks, Howard Schultz, who understood that he was creating an experience, not selling a product. He has been successful at seeing the value of his staff, including emphasizing hiring practices to create a diversified, inclusive staff that attract customers. New York Yankees shortstop & captain, Derek Jeter, who played 20 seasons in "the pinstripes". Jeter stands out as a role model because of his old-school approach: Never offer excuses or give less than maximum effort.

See if your thoughts on which dominant leadership style for each of these extraordinary people match mine at the end of this article.

Now that you have matched these inspirational leaders with their dominant leadership styles, which leadership style are you? And by the way, your dominant leadership style already exists. It is what you are most comfortable with and very well may incorporate elements from all six of these styles. It is common for leaders to have one dominant style and minor elements from other styles. This is beneficial because it allows you to relate to the vast majority of individuals.

To use myself as an example, it is clear to me and others that my dominant leadership style is coaching. This style's key element involves developing people for future leadership roles along with the ability to attract and retain the best individual performers and have them work as a team towards a common vision. Having two children with higher than average skill sets in sports encouraged me to get involved with their various teams. Rising through the ranks of many of their sports organizations in roles including team manager, club executive and most importantly, coaching. My passion for coaching sports dreaded opportunities for me to coach top athletes and teams and to build coaching staffs that would ensure the team's highest level of success, including in one case, a world championship for a Canadian women's roller hockey team on an international stage. One of the top priorities of a coach, either in sports, business, politics or other aspects of life, is the ability to help build strong team leaders. This team of leaders helps ensure members of the team can relate to different leadership styles. Consider attracting other leaders for your team that have different dominant leadership styles from your own. This will mitigate your weaknesses and support your strengths.

This leverages the strengths of your collective leadership abilities and strengthens the overall team.

Discovering and utilizing your dominant leadership style, combined with allowing your authentic self to come through, will encourage other leaders and members of your collective team to do the same. If you are passionate, be passionate. If you are emotional, be emotional. Humans truly connect with each other on a personal level, not a business level. You don't have to be "best buds" but you must have at least a few human elements in common in order to effectively work together with individuals and effectively lead. Engage feelings as well as facts. Do not try to be someone you are not. Garner the leadership style that is already in you. To be an accomplished leader, you must understand each individual's role within your team. This includes both team leaders and team players. Understanding each team player is most easily achieved by opening up and sharing yourself, if this is your style. You will create a stronger and deeper relationship with those around you, creating a dynamic and winning team and develop future leaders in the process.

When you are being the natural you, you will feel energized, balanced, inspired and inspiring. You will have the ability to draw freely and deliberately from your personality, strengths and values in order to lead others. You will motivate, inspire, and propel people and teams forward to new levels of success in all aspects of their lives. Through my experiences, I have become fully aware that being your self is not a risk, it's an opportunity. Don't ever let anyone tell you otherwise.

> *"Leadership simply begins with the courage to be yourself. So everyone else can be, too."* Umair Hague, Author and Economist

Leadership Quality #3: Be a Source of Positivity and Inspiration

Give some thought to leaders you've admired over time, in business and also in your personal life. Think of individuals that have made a positive impact on you. This could be a relative, a coach, a teacher or coworker or boss. What you'll discover is that these individuals are leaders. Although they may possess some natural leadership abilities, they have also spent time learning and refining their leadership skills. They will have connected with you on several levels. One key to their being an inspiration and admired leader is to exude positivity and passionately inspire those around them. How you treat others is as important as how you dress, act and carry yourself. Leading by example is an important part of leadership.

Human nature propels us to place ourselves in environments with people that make us feel good. Those types of people raise the energy level in a room just by entering it. A leader's appearance and how they carry themselves in a very confident manner, without arrogance, exudes likability. Great leaders make others feel that they contribute and make a difference to an important cause. They inspire people to be and do their absolute best. You can take this same approach.

Several years removed from active sports coaching, I had a young man I had on one of my teams in his late teens approach me in the local shopping mall. He addressed me as 'Coach' and proceeded to tell me how successful he had been in gaining access to the university of his choice, in part because of a scholarship in his chosen sport. He shared how his learning's early on from me and our coaching staff had made such a positive impact in his life. He related how all our coaching came together for him. This included the disciplined approach of showing up at the arena on time, in game day dress attire, having spent the day preparing by eating the right foods, having proper rest and ensuring his equipment was in top shape, as his mind and body were from hours of preparation. He learned from us that commitment, dedication and focus were learned skills that he could use in other areas of his life. Inspiring others to be the best they can be, to set lofty and achievable goals, giving them the tools and knowledge to be successful, is within you as a strong leader.

Now, the much anticipated quiz portion of my article. Well, not really, but let's see how your perception of these leaders' dominant styles compare mine. I will refrain from justifying my choices, since you do not have an opportunity to defend yours. However, I am always up for a nice hot tea and a spirited conversation on the subject.

Bono - Visionary

Dali Lama - Affiliative

Angelina Jolie - Democratic

Howard Schultz - Coaching

Derek Jeter - Pacesetting

Be the leader you're capable of. Harness your natural, personal and fantastic leadership style and empower others along the way to greatness. And remember,

> "Great leaders don't set out to be a leader…they set out to make a difference. It's never about the role, always about the goal"
>
> Richard Branson

References:

1. Deloitte University

Uncovering talent; A new model of inclusion

Written by: Kenji Yoshino, Chief Justice Earl Warren Professor of Constitutional Law, NYU School of Law

Christie Smith, Managing Principal, Deloitte University Leadership Center for Inclusion, Deloitte LLP

Updated December 6, 2013

2. The Harvard Business Review published research in 2000 by author and psychologist Daniel Goleman

3. The World's 50 Greatest Leaders (2014) by Fortune Editors March 20, 2014

Rick Denley

A courageous sales executive with extensive background in successful sales growth strategies and execution. A proven ability to align sales goals with that of the company goals. A natural leader who combines coaching tactics with real world experience to create successful, winning teams. Working at a Director level, Rick's career has seen him leading Canadian divisions for multi-nationals based in Japan (Matsushita Group), France, (Schneider), USA (Emerson), and Germany (Phoenix Contact). In 2009, during the difficult days for the manufacturing sector, Rick took on a challenging role as General Manager for a failing systems integrator (Soft Design Automation) and successfully right sized and returned organization to profitability by creating a new revenue stream, and then successfully completed the sale of the organization to a larger firm (JMP Engineering). As a board of director member, Rick took on an advisory role with different committees within the Canadian Manufacturers and Exporters Group, including the membership growth group driving membership to all time high levels. Rick contributed to numerous initiatives essential to sustaining and growing the CME's key programs. Rick is applying his years of leadership learning and success and developing a leadership presentation for release shortly.

Becoming the Reawakened Spirit Within

~

By Rita Aldo Rasi

Spiritual awareness brings strength to the heart and confidence to the mind.

It nourishes and expands, becoming the solid anchor during the worst of storms and the beacon of light that shines throughout your life.

Raised in a typical middle class, Roman Catholic Italian family, living life organically, and to its fullest was not within the mindset tailored to our daily lives or aspirations.

Life was boisterous and full, with family, work, love, work, and religion. Did I say, work? Working hard was instilled in our every waking moment, with a family run business that dictated all family discussions, vacations and spare moment. It was instilled within us early on, to work through and warrior on through most hardships, sickness and adolescent laziness. The true immigrant rule of getting ahead, check the handbook!

As a free spirited, challenging and rebellious child, instilling rules proved to be a difficult and an aurous task for my parents, who had little time to rein in their last-born.

Back in the day, challenging their youngest with the modern luxuries of Internet, brainteasers, or Learning Centres of course, simply just did not exist. So my parents jumped at the idea of a Martial Arts class in a Dojo with a strict Japanese Sensei with classes taught in the back of our church that did become my place of refuge.

Martial arts was not only a fantastic facet for my energies, but a training ground for meditation, self-observance, and mental training that would assist in almost every aspect of my life. Little did I know then, that this would become my saviour and place of mental, spiritual and physical solace.

Although my narrative could have ultimately become anything I chose it to be, growing up and fitting in was a mandate in my home. I felt compelled to fulfill my family's approach of a traditional family, marriage, and home with all of the trappings of a middle class life.

As life happened, I found myself repeatedly faced with hardship breaking me down to my very core. It was in these moments of rock bottom, that I came to terms with my inner most spirit. Each hardship caused another layer to be peeled open to reveal the naked spirit in its most venerable state.

Through my own examples of abuse, divorce, single motherhood, financial devastation, sickness, depression, legal arbitration, mediation and family tragedies I marched on as this was the only option. Yet again, I felt compelled to resort deeper to my martial arts discipline. Looking back to what each experience has given me value to what I was experiencing, what I was learning, and how it all affected me and those around me.

During those powerful moments and lessons, I learned to embrace the very silence that allowed my mind to calm down, breathe and expand. Alone that silence became my best friend, fuelling my thoughts, dreams and aspirations connecting with my inner spirit and my inner child once again.

Now was the time to become reawakened with my inner spirit and the vibrant light that still glowed abet dim but was there nevertheless.

Invariably, we all live on the primary principle that great things will happen to good people who consistently do good things. Unfortunately, that is not always the case. However, in saying that and not sounding too dismal, remember it is in the hardship that gives us and the knowledge, the lessons and the experience to learn and grow, to expand your spirit.

It has been said that those who have truthfully experienced the varying depth of darkness, can truly appreciate and embrace the light.

I am a firm believer that ordinary people can do extraordinary things, once they start believing they can and commence to be confident in their own being. The concept that each and every one of us has within us, a unique version of genius, directs the mindset that it just needs to be awakened and unleashed.

To become re-awakened you must be willing to absorb and infuse this new thought process actively in your life. Here three changes you can make that will be life changing, I know this, as it has changed mine, and continues to allow me to evolve.

1. LIVE LIFE IN BOLD

Life in general is to be lived, and we seem to live life postponing our aspirations rather than truly living. Most of us live each day as if we have all of the time in the world or we have extra days on hold. Be Bold people!

We are passionate as to what we want to do one day, but always share the stories of when things slow down, kids are grown, or when I retire never giving any thought that our days are truly numbered. Ideally we don't have any extra days than those that we are given on this earth. Serve them well and make each and every day count for each of the 24hours of each day you are given.

Live life boldly, fiercely and with a mission to your dreams. We are meant to seize the moment and live our lives to the utmost, ensuring we are present and truly living inside and out.

If we were to live each day as a living example of what the best life for you would be.

What would you do?

What would you include?

What would you change?

More importantly what would you eliminate?

How would you start each day and how would it differ from your regular day?

Hard hitting questions? No, merely a new thought process that can be changed each day by 1 degree, or percentage that changes your direction. Each day, 1 degree of change and your landscape and perspective will unquestionably be altered.

    1. Make your life list not your bucket list.

2. Plan each day to step outside your normal path.

3. Review your list often and truly live it.

4. Live it boldly as the person you like to be around.

The philosophy of living each day as your last allows us to embrace the thought process that we truly do not have much input in the main variables of our own narrative.

Living boldly is ideally throwing out the mindset of residing within your comfort zone and allowing oneself to dive in at the deep end, lending room for true growth and new experiences.

Why not live life in total awesomeness?

Unleashing your awesome is easy once you allow yourself to let go of the traditional thought process and allow for change, allow for growth, and allow for an amazing life to unfold.

"No matter what people tell you, words and ideas can change the world."

~Robin Williams

"Be yourself; everyone else is already taken."

~Oscar Wilde

Lesson here is- to make the bold choices that propel the change in yourself that you allow you to grow outside your comfort zone and open to a new and exciting life!

2. LIVE LIFE IN KNOWLEDGE

To many, ignorance may be bliss, but it never paved the road to success and true well-being, nor has it ever held the answers to many of society's relevant issues.

Regardless of your age, gender, race, or stature in life, education is the key to not only move toward your goals and/or dreams, but to open you up to an expanding and changing world. How do you make the necessary changes to embrace new knowledge? Good question!

Try to allocate an hour to your future everyday with any sort of topic that expands your current mindset. Learning from a variable of arenas that will invariably expands your mind. How exciting?

Read a book a month, take online courses, learn through audio tapes, or merely subscribe to a newsletter, or through your mentor's in social media.

As humans, we are learning machines that are constantly evolving and changing from a young age, it is literally in our genetics. Utilizing a mere 10% of our brains, we are functioning closer to our true potential when we are continually increasing our awareness, adapting, adjusting and approaching new techniques to better our life and ourselves.

Actively learning can be not only be socially invigorating, but will also greatly improve memory and cognitive abilities to support mental wellness later in life. Embracing new ideas, new mindsets and concepts is in actuality embracing change.

As life is continuously transforming, change is inevitable and can propel you into unknown territory without a handbook. Seeking knowledge is a mindset of behaviours that allow us to succeed in an ever-changing environment. In all aspects of our professional and personal lives change surrounds us and allows for growth. Change requires learning and ultimately, there is no learning without change.

So open up your minds and live in the knowledge that is in abundance and infuse a whole new world of informational transformation.

"Never regard study as a duty but as an enviable opportunity to learn to know the liberating influence of beauty in the realm of the spirit for

your own personal joy and to the profit of the community to which your later works belong."

~Albert Einstein

"Live as if you were to die tomorrow. Learn as if you were to live forever."

~ Mahatma Gandhi

Lesson here is- to allow yourself to openly seek knowledge in an ever changing world that will invariably allow you to expand your mind, grow your horizons and embrace all dreams with confidence.

3. LIVE LIFE IN LOVE

Children arrive more highly evolved in their ability to love than their older adult counterparts, as they are always ready to love, like, enjoy, smile and be happy. However as we grow, we are taught to contain ourselves and to calm the wildness of our inner child.

Do you remember a time when jumping up and down and clapping was a wonderful expression of happiness? We are taught to remain calm, to be thoughtful but hide our feelings of exuberance to become refrained in our daily lives. I say Hell No! Tap into your inner child!

Becoming actively loving, and compassionate every single day towards all of those around you, opens your landscape to a positive world with loving response in return. Random acts of kindness, love and compassion is a born disposition, which we should all embrace and emulate in our daily lives.

The common philosophy of successful people, are given courage to live out that ideology that we all deep down crave to live in happiness and contentment. This in turn, promotes extraordinary levels of confidence as they are aware that being true to themselves and can do so in a compassionate way.

Daily practice in creating a love directed mind-set ironically makes you feel more loved! Imagine that? Why not create your own love reservoir spreading love each and every day that bounces back to you, that will build your happiness without reservation?

Think love, be love and become loving.

"Spread love everywhere you go. Let no one ever come to you without leaving happier."

~Mother Teresa

"I offer you peace. I offer you love. I offer you friendship. I see your beauty. I hear your need. I feel your feelings. My wisdom flows from the Highest Source. I salute that Source in you. Let us work together for unity and love."

~Mahatma Gandhi

Lesson here is- to reawaken that inner spirit that yearns for love, for a full life, for excitement and to reside in a loving world of compassion!

You can write or rewrite your own ending as your narrative can be whatever you want it to be, and aspire to be. Why not do something amazing? I know you can, if I can!

Today I live my life in Rita-vision. With the life concept that being knowledgeable, seeking bold excellence and compassionately loving each other will never goes out of style. Success didn't look for me, I found it, when I became truthfully aligned with my inner spirit. True success is when preparation meets opportunity.

My hope as you finish my chapter, that I have somehow inspired you to join me in living a life seeking knowledge, living compassionately in love and becoming unapologetically bold to live organically unique on our confident path.

Congratulations!

You are now becoming the Reawaken Spirit Warrior....

Sat nam!

Rita Aldo Rasi

Rita Aldo Rasi is an Education Director, Trainer, Author, Blogger, NLP Practitioner, Spiritual and Startegic Life Coach, Mother and student of life, specializing in Spirituality, Wellness and Strategic Transformational Growth in Mind, Body and Soul. For years, Rita was European trained in the beauty and cosmeceutical industries where she taught Advanced Medical Aesthetics, Aromatherapy, Body Therapy and Medical Aesthetics focusing on inventive health and naturopathic wellness. Having directed, and instructed in 6 of the leading Aesthetic Private Schools and Career Colleges in the greater Toronto area, as well as Vancouver, BC, Rita has an impressive understanding of the protocols and industry standards for educating with a purpose. Establishing many accreditations and writing innovative curriculums within the PCC sector for the Ministry of Education, Rita has also facilitated the opening of many new schools across Canada and Vancouver. Education has always been the main directive and driving force in Rita's career. She has been able to serve her motto and mission of "Knowledge is Power, Action is the Catalyst".

Aspire to expand your knowledge, boldly expand your boundaries and unleash the colorful reality of your dreams with love and compassion ~Rita Aldo Rasi

In this focus, her drive has always been to become a channel of education, leading those to the knowledge and training they require for self-improvement, self-awareness and growth.

Rita currently trains individuals who seek to live boldly, seeking knowledge and in love with life using online courses and magazine, seminars and retreats all over the globe.

As the founder and CEO of Girltalk Enterprises Inc. (2009), Rita runs her online magazine – www.Mavensmag.com #mavensmag, her life coaching practice her pet project - UUA www.unleashurawesome.com retreats and events as well as her "Reawaken the Spirit Warrior" book and courses #spiritwarrior.

You can reach Rita at:

Email: info@mavensmag.com or rialdo@hotmail.com

Website: www.mavensmag.com

Project: www.unleashurawesome.com

The Eagle In You

~

By Steve Kerr

"It's only when you're aiming high, you spread your wings and truly fly!" skerr

In all my years of living on this earth, I have come to the realization that,

"It's not the beginning that makes a man but his ending." skerr

I know you have been faced with many challenges. Perhaps you are going though some issues right now but with all due respect, I do not wish to hear about your sob story of why you cannot succeed. I have learned every story that you have about "woe is me," there is someone that overcame your situation and worse. Here are two KEY principles you must adapt to, in order to excel.

The first Key principle is your **perception** and second is your **faith** in believing you can overcome. All the skills of success can be learned, but with the knowledge alone it is not enough. You have to put your knowledge into practice. The powerful thing about success is the universe is there to assist you. The universe is built on the principle of success and increase. The animal kingdom and the plant kingdom thrive by multiplication. Humanity did not begin with 7 billion people but that is where we are now because nature is designed to expand. All of creation has an innate will to live and grow but how you grow is determined by the seeds you plant.

Although your brain has matured, and your head is no longer getting any bigger yet your mind is forever expanding with knowledge. Man cannot quantify as to how much capacity is in our mental storage space but the universe is waiting for your expansion. It is waiting for you to achieve the success of your heart's desire. It is waiting for you to discover your passion and purpose. Anthony Robins, who is a motivational guru said to "wake the giant in you". I say to you,

"It's time for you to take flight because there is an eagle in you!"

My friend James Erdt, who is the Chief Architect of Dynamo Entrepreneur, has a passion for eagles. I too share that passion for more than one reason, so let me tell you a story using my passion.

Majestic Flight

On a beautiful sunny spring day, high on the side of a mountain, an eaglet was born. To keep the story in the proper context, he was hatched along with his sister but this story is about the male eagle and his journey to success. The mother and father eagles agreed to name the male eagle James. From birth, James was surrounded by the love of his parents and the warmth and security of his home, the nest. In a nutshell life was good and grand. With his youthful feathers, James looked like a huge cotton ball. Being high in the mountains, as a young eaglet James' parents took turns covering him to protect him from the cold reality of life (the wind). While one parent sat and kept him warm, the other brought fresh meat that was chewed, swallowed and regurgitated for James to consume. James just had to open his mouth and presto, he was full. As I said before James had a good life with no worries.

As time progressed and the seasons changed from spring to summer, James continued to be fed. James lived off of the diet of regurgitated flesh of fish and small rodents like rabbits, ground squirrels and snakes. One day James was very hungry and he was waiting patiently for his mother to return to deposit his food down his throat but things were different. James perceived that things were business as usual but times had changed and so must James. Just like seasons change with time, James had not yet learned he had to flow with the seasons. James was older and strong enough to learn how to tear his food for himself. James's mother did arrive on time but this time with a live fish in her beak. She dropped the fish in the nest and the fish began to flutter and gasp as if it was trying to breathe. James ignored the fish and hopped over to his mother and opened his mouth for his routine meal but his mother squawked at him and pushed him with her beak towards the foreign object. James was totally confused about what was to happen so his mother demonstrated by holding the fish down with her powerful talons. Piercing the flesh of the fish with her needle like beak, she tore a small piece of flesh off the fish and spat it near the claws of her son. James bent down and his sense of smell kicked in. Something inside told him "food." He picked up the small portion of fish and swallowed it. James recognized the familiar taste and gobbled up everything his mother threw at him.

This type of feeding went on for approximately two weeks. James' faith was in his parents ability to bring and tear meat for him to devour. Like before, time had progressed and James had to graduate from this style of feeding as he did before. His parents just simply brought the meal, dropped it in the nest and flew away. They did not stick around to listen to the complaints of James. James remembered seeing his mother pierce her claws into the prey for stability as she ripped small pieces of meat for him to consume. James knew he had to do the tearing for himself because there was no one around to do the tearing for him. With his knowledge and newly discovered strength, James took action and was very successful. In no time his belly was satisfied. James was feeling great about his accomplishments. He would strut around the nest as if he was King of the skies, then nestle down into his cozy nest for a nap.

When his parents came and saw James lazing around the house, they took drastic measures in their hands. They removed all the feathers and everything that made the home comfortable. Picture yourself laying down on your expensive Craftmatic Adjustable Bed and someone comes in your bedroom and removes all the cushions and leaves just the springs. That is what James was now experiencing. James was no longer comfortable laying down. In fact, James spent most of his time on his feet (claws)

The wind slowly blew on James's body and face. It was the first time he was experiencing the harshness of life. When James thought it could not get any worse, the wind picked up to the point where he slowly lost all his feathers. His parents started to stay away for longer periods of time so James could not rely on his parents to shield him from the frigid temperature of the mountain wind. James felt like he was going to die but death did not come. What came was a tougher outer skin that was forged from the rugged air of the mountains.

Weeks past and the wind kept blowing but James was no longer affected by the cold anymore. It was as if his body became numb to the affects of the cold air. Standing most of the day increased James' muscle around his talons and he also grew brand new feathers. This time these feathers were black, waterproof and strong. James now looked like his parents. His body had a dark sheen and it glistened from the reflection of the sun. The feathers on his head were completely white. James' eyes were yellow and black. He had the ability to see moving objects miles away. Being a male eagle, James would grow as tall as his dad but for now he was one third the size and feeling very proud of himself.

One day, while his father hunted, James was walking on the rim of the nest. His mother observed James, from a distance, as she perched on a nearby ledge. James kept walking in a circle, flapping his wings and testing out his newly found long distance vision. Many days, he watched his parents leave the nest by flapping their wings so James started emulating his parents and exercising his right to be an Eagle. James would spread his wings out to the max potential and hold it there. It was as if he was Rocky Balboa after he sprinted up the stairs and held his hands up in victory. In the background, you heard the music "The Eye of The Tiger". In this case it was The Eye of The Eagle and James was that eagle. Suddenly a stronger gust of wind came from beneath him and took him by surprise. The wind came under him like a thief that was a purse snatcher. The wind grabbed his open wings and elevated him slowly like a hydraulic lift. In fear, James reacted by digging his talons into the rim of his nest to refrain from going air born. The updraft was so strong, it caused James to lift the corner of his nest above its resting place. As quick as the gust came, it subsided and the nest was back in its rightful place.

The entire event lasted seconds but was under the watchful eye of his mother and mother eagle knew it was time to take James to another dimension of training. Mom joined James in the nest and he was happy to see her. She perched on the south side of the rim of the nest while James was on the far north. It was obvious this nest was not your average size robin's nest. The size of the nest was approximately 4 feet in diameter. James was so happy to see his mother, he continued to spread his wings as if he was showing off for her. When his back was turned, his mother swiftly but quietly moved across the centre of the nest and using her powerful wings, knocked James out of the nest. For the first time in his life, James was air born and separated from his home. Immediately James began to plummet towards the base of the mountain. With fear James franticly fluttered his wings in panic. Even though he was still falling, James fluttering slowed down his descent. It was as if James was a person in deep water and discovered he did not know how to swim. James was drowning slowly.

When his mother realized James was not going to recover from his free fall, she reacted by lowering her head forward and leaping out of the nest with her wings folded close to her body. His mother darted out of the nest like a bullet exiting the barrel of a pistol. Because of her arrow dynamic posture, she caught up to James in no time. She swooped beneath him, opened her wings like a parachute and nestled him gently on her back. Without damaging his mother severely, James dug his talons into the feathers of his mother's back like a drowning man gripping to a life preserver. With the experience of mother eagle, she used the current of the wind and continued soaring in a circular motion until she arrived back safely in the nest. After overcoming his initial fear, James enjoyed the ride and view of his new playground. After many trials and errors, James was no longer afraid of being knocked out of his nest. Matter of fact he invited it. James replaced his fear with courage. He became like an experienced skydiver back flipping out of an open airplane. He would yell, "Whoo hoo" as he descended and waited for his mother to catch up and rest him upon her back.

On a bright sunny, day when James thought his mother was going to knock him out of the nest, instead, she opened her wings and elevated upon the breath of the air like a red helium balloon that lost the grip of a child. She started to fly away from the nest. She looked back as if she was saying to James, "What are you waiting for, let's go! Be like Nike and Just Do It." James did not want to get left behind so he leapt up, spread his wings and began to chase his mother like a dog chasing a frisbee. Just like that James was airborne and flying with authority. He was feeling really good about what he had achieved. Like a child learning to ride a bike for the first time, James looked for his parents approval. They flew together and disappeared over the top of the mountain and began to descend on the other side towards the sea. His next lesson was to learn how to hunt for himself but that is another story for another day.

CONCLUSION

If you put a fish in water, it will swim. Put a bird in the sky and it will learn how to fly. That is because it is in its domain. It is in its natural element to succeed. I am here to tell you, "It is not a matter of how you begin or the challenges you face along the way, but the completion of your journey. Up until this point, you have not gained your desired success because of your perception. You don't believe success is for you! You perceive it is for others and you give yourself reasons to fail or remain in poverty.

"It's not the beginning that makes a man but the ending" skerr

You need to have that faith that there is an eagle in you that is waiting to be pushed out of his comfort zone. There is an eagle in you that desire to rise above every challenge that nature can throw at him. The Bald Eagle is the Majestic Chief of the sky, there is no other bird nor will there be any other bird that can achieve like the eagle in its domain. The Eagle was created to be the King of the skies. His wings will never fail him. He has the SKILL to fly beneath the storm, the POWER to soar above the storm and the STRENGTH to go through the storm. It is just a matter of Choice for the eagle. Poverty cannot keep you down unless you choose to remain there. Drug and Alcohol addictions cannot keep you from soaring. They were challenges to build your character. The discomforts you are facing is merely preparing you for greater challenges. This is your season to rise. This is your season to succeed. This is your season to WIN! James was knocked out of his comfort zone but he kept flapping his wings until his wings grew stronger and stronger to conquer the skies. There is an eagle in you and it is ready for the hunt for success. Take Action NOW and make it happen because when you take action, the universe will respond and make room for you. Don't ever forget......*It's Only When You're Aiming High, You Spread Your Wings And Truly Fly"* skerr

Steve Kerr

STEVE KERR is one of the world's international and inspirational speakers. He has a captivating personality and highly sought-after resource in business and professional circles. STEVE KERR offer his skills towards the start up of a small business, non-profit and community leaders from all sectors of society, looking to expand opportunity. With over 30 years of experience STEVE KERR has studied how to ignite the fire (ability) in you so you can achieve your maximum potential. STEVE is a father of seven children, a track and field coach and a mentor to many to improve their spiritual, mental and physical well-being. He skillfully weaves the practical POWER OF WORDS with his amazing storytelling ability to awaken the GREATNESS that is in you so you can change the world in a positive way. STEVE KERR is an Author of the book "Who Am I". With his proven system called M.A.P.P.S., he will teach you to "Aim High…..Spread Wings…..Fly!!!!" STEVE KERR received an award from Toast Master International as a component communicator. He also finished 3rd in the 2016 DYNAMO speaker talent search. He is one of the trainers of Speakers University. By overcoming the fear of public speaking STEVE has been a mentor to many political figures and to empower others to be civically engaged in their community.

Dedication To Success Is A Choice

~

By Tracey McLeod

You've held your breath, endured countless sleepless nights and taken the first step to becoming an entrepreneur. Let's review a few points that have made a difference in my journey in hopes it will assist you, in yours.

MINDSET

The question that must be asked first is, do you believe you can do this? Do you have what it takes to become a successful entrepreneur? The answers to these questions will guide you through your daily routines and will either elevate or sabotage your efforts. Time to dig deep here, what do you believe? Personal mindset will steer the ship. What are your core beliefs? What do you believe is important? The power of thought and their influence warrant respect and acknowledgment at all times. Many of us will have different experiences both personally and professionally and it's the sum total of these experiences which will influence beliefs. I have been in both positive and negative work environments. I tend to do my best when the environment and my beliefs are in line with each other. Inner peace for me, occurs when the business I am working is in line with my authentic self. You are truly special – embrace your magic and you will shine.

Open yourself up to opportunity. Confess you are human and as such need help. No need to work in a silo. The benefits of those around you offering support may be exactly what you need on a challenging day. Consciously surround yourself with positive people who are driven and successful. The exchange of energy is powerful and never to be underestimated. Successful people often want others to succeed as well. Stories about what has propelled them to reach their successes are willingly exchanged with great pride with the undercurrent of desire to help others. A network of positive energy shared with enthusiasm and honesty will help fuel your days. Collaboration can be very beneficial as there are ample opportunities for an exchange of skill sets assisting all within network. History suggests when you help people what you get in return a.k.a. ROI is far greater than your initial investment. Much will be learned through acts of kindness and generosity.

Abundance or Famine, in business often dominates your mindset and will play a major role in how you conduct business. Famine is fear based and can create a silo, top secret, paranoid, there's not enough to survive so I have to get mine, mentality. While no one can debate the importance of getting the sale, closing the deal or acquiring a new client how we do that can often be felt and interpreted by your prospective client. Imagine if your will these two scenarios and you decide for yourself how they play out and who you'd want to do business with.

Gavin a.k.a. famine mentality. Gavin is a smart business man. He believes he's always 1 step away from certain demise. He knows his business inside and out yet when delivering message to prospects he is intense and charges through information like the running of the bulls. He makes any promise he has to, regardless if he can deliver or not, just so he can close this deal. He speaks poorly of his competition and believes in doing so allows him to be seen as the cream of the crop. In reality, he may be sending the air of desperation to his potential clients and runs the risk of being interpreted as a disrespectful bully who is only interested in closing the deal. The belief that in order for your business to survive others must perish rarely is the case. This intensity may feed a lack of trust and uncertainty when the time comes for client to decide whom they want to work with.

Leon a.k.a. abundance. Possess confidence and knowledge. Takes the time to learn if he is the best choice for potential client and makes recommendations based on what is learned. If he is the best fit, then he proceeds to explain his strengths and why they align with prospects needs. If, however; Leon knows he's not the best fit, he then refers client onto someone who is. Does he lose the sale – yes? Is he remembered by clients and the businesses to whom he sent this client to – yes? The truth is none of us can be all things to all people. If you are good at what you do and have clients' needs as your priority you will earn the respect on the streets and in business. Your name and integrity is something within your control at all times. Strategy and open communication can build your referral network. Be aware and watchful that all of those trusted within your circle are operating by the same code of ethics. Don't sell yourself short – know your strengths and play to them. Often there is more than enough business for everyone to prosper. Be clear on the difference between famine and abundance. Deliver the message you are proud to stand behind when speaking with prospects and peers.

When I opened myself up to opportunity and people it created a space for me. With this space a business was created and is run mirroring what's important to me along with the confidence in abundance for all. Beliefs steer my ship and can steer yours as well. I truly believe you will always prove yourself right no matter what you believe. Pay close attention to your beliefs and take time to really know what they are. Beliefs just may be the difference between your struggle and your success.

LEARNING

In real estate you often hear location, location, location. As an entrepreneur may I suggest network, network, network! Networking has endless benefits. Now is the time to meet like minded individuals dedicated to their success and motivated by the success of others. If you have not found a mentor here is a great place to look. Stories shared of each other's successes and challenges encourages a greater understanding of options and solutions. The ability to brainstorm with the elite will foster your confidence, create a springboard for growth and opportunity.

Education and development can take place when you commit to reading, workshops, and taking extra courses on topics that assist you in positioning your business on the curve for the future. Learning goes a long away in keeping that pilot light lit and the spark of enthusiasm shining bright.

Believe in yourself and invest in yourself. You're an amazing and exciting mind that has something so unique and so special, only you can deliver. Learning has a beginning but no end. Embrace your journey of discovery and expansion. Learning leads to a metamorphosis only you can create and live. Breathe in knowledge, breathe out your vision.

COMMITMENT TO ACTION

It is easy to have your days consumed with "busy work". It's important to install a measurement tool or metric to ensure you are moving towards your goals and not just simply moving. Time management must be mastered in order to effectively maximize time and effort.

Prioritize all necessary activities then schedule them in your calendar. Remain fluid and flexible. Order of activities may need to shift based on daily needs, but it's important to remain dedicated to all points of interest in your day. As business picks up your criteria may shift again from learning and planning to learning and implementing to learning and making money. A phrase we often hear in business is, "Plan your work and work your plan". Habits are formed through repetition and it's important to ensure the most effective habits are being formed.

Action and success need to be measured daily, weekly, monthly, quarterly, and yearly in order to see patterns arising that lead to or distract you from your goals and ultimately success. Tracking actions can be monitored in a spreadsheet. Track number of calls, new networks built, progress with next steps booked, increase in number of potential clients, increase in clients, sales growth, healthy margins and your ultimate goal achieved. Ensure that you are simply not just creating paperwork. Increase your chances for new business and clients. The beginning can be filled with uncertainty, but build a plan that is measurable and creates a clear visual where you are heading and it just may give you a little more peace of mind along the way. If non-productive activities are consuming your time then you should be able to see this pattern, correct it and get you back on the track to success.

Motivation spawns action – action spawns results. Build your momentum and watch your snowball start small and grow to a bolder. No judgement, no self-criticizing, simply assess and correct each step of the way. The best lessons learned are often through making mistakes so don't be afraid to make some along the way, we all have. Learn what you can, adjust and move on. No need to wallow or stall future progress. Constant movement constant reinforcement. As your habits are formed and you can visually see you are doing the work and getting closer to goals you can stay motivated, never arrogant, and get excited about what you are creating and learning along the way. Measure in absolute not interpretations – number of meetings, next steps leading to decision, number of sales, number of repeat clients, number of contacts in industry that can propel you forward. Find a problem that affects many and solve it. Make sure you target your attention to those affected then let them know have the solution. It's time to take your idea from thought to snowball to a boulder!!!

Thought, action, belief, reaction are all a choice we have every moment of every day. We have the ability to make these choices for ourselves. What do you believe? Is success within your grasp? Can you create success? Are you dedicated to continual learning and improvement? Are you flexible and fluid to adjust to what is needed? Are you motivated? Are you committed to action that will bring you to your goals and surpass them? Are you ready to be an entrepreneur? Creator of your destiny and Captain of your ship. Success has many definitions – one definition no more right than the other. Know what your definition is. Align your beliefs, your time, your business, and your actions with your definition of success. Monitor every step of the way to ensure you are getting closer to realizing your dreams every week. Your true potential is as powerful as your beliefs. It's time to prove you're right and pave the way to your dreams and beyond. Here's to you and your new future!!

Tracey McLeod

20 years media experience holding positions as a member on the Board of Directors, Copywriter, Producer, On-Air host, Freelance Writer and Advertising Sales Executive. Advertising sales experience spans Online, TV, Radio, and print in one of Canada's' largest Newspapers. Client focus and responsibilities have ranged from no list/no clients - sink or swim on a few occasions, small local business, unions, education, automotive, government, international education, broadcast, national retail, 100% agency and solely responsible for all major financial institutions in Canada. Multi award winning Account Executive amongst peers in all markets across Canada and recognized at the International Level for executions that were team efforts that I had the privilege to lead and be part of. Strictly from a writing standpoint was responsible for my own column in a magazine that was published quarterly and was a proud part of this for many years. I've written for a number of different papers ranging in content from event coverage, restaurant reviews to lifestyle and general interest. Possess a passion for life, writing, business and believe in the importance of motivating and helping others.

Latha,

May you find your greatest blessings in your pain & glory.

May you be blessed with all your desires and dreams.

With Love
Zoë Lucy

Wisdom From Within

~

By Zak Lioutas

Sleepless nights.

Mind wandering days

Confusion, disconnect, unworthiness, lack, pain, suffering lingering in my heart.

There must be a better way.

Why do I always go down the same path of pain?

Why am I revisiting the same story of yesterday into today?

Why is my heart so heavy?

AM I TO BE LIVING THIS PAINFUL LIFE FOREVER?

Hello God, are you listening?

It wasn't a matter if God was listening, the real question was, am I listening. It was me that was putting myself through all the pain, the suffering, the anger, resentment and disregard; it had nothing to do with the universe. I was the director of my life, the universe supported me in all ways, regardless if I took the wrong path, there was a lesson attached to the pain realizing that was the path I was meant to travel. It's a path that teaches us a deeper sense of self. When I travelled on the righteous path, there were lessons along with gifts rewarding me for spreading the love as intended by the cosmos.

When the words came streaming down to me, God gave me the best wisdom.

My love, you are precious know that.

What you are experiencing is the lesson of your heart and how big and bright it is.

I brought you to earth to be glorious, abundant, wealthy and accepting of the most difficult journeys you have passed, the real issue is you're holding onto more pain then glorious new beginnings of love and all the amazingness you have achieved in this lifetime.

The lesson was a painful one, and the wisdom profound in how the universe viewed life, I have never looked at it that way. It was time I change my perception of life and how I viewed it. It's time to glance at everything as a lesson on a soulful level in learning a deeper sense of myself, learning that it can be difficult and enlightening all at the same time, that life was about duality.

Asking myself the difficult questions.

Why did I travel down certain paths?

Why did I date the men I was dating?

Why did I allow others to treat me with disrespect?

Why at times didn't I speak up?

Why haven't I recognized my worth and value to humanity?

Why am I afraid to succeed in the story of life?

The questions came seeping through each and every tear. WHY?

After many years of depression, anxiety, fears I forgot who ME was. I reflected on my childhood. What did I do for fun as a child, into my teens, 20's, 30's and beyond. As I was remising through my life, I cried every tear of pain. In my teens I felt so out of place in the world, I couldn't explain who I truly was and when I did, I was told not to mention anything, being misunderstood in many ways. My universal gifts were a curse, rather than a blessing.

In my 20's I went through thyroid cancer, no surprise to the soul having a difficult time expressing me again. Depression repeating itself, the vicious cycle was something that always found me. When I expressed a part of my universal gifts and the wisdom I received in taking care of my health, I was looked at sideways, dodging being admitted into the psychiatric ward by instantly hearing my spirit guides tell me to stop and walk away. Was this gift really a curse or a blessing? Once again confusion arose and pain felt more debilitating than I could handle. Here I was in my 20's just passing through a massive phase in my life, letting go of all my addictions from my teenage years now experiencing what felt like adult illnesses.

As I was running away from the outside world, my inside world taught me lessons. Falling down into the darkness of depression the light felt difficult to see. Again the questions would start to linger in my mind but now it wasn't why me, it was what am I going to do to change all this?

What is it, I want to do?

How is it, I want to shine?

What do I want to receive from this story they call life?

Who are the people, I want to work and surround myself with?

The questions were streaming down to me, as the light started to shine within me mirroring my outside world. Starting to feel once again there is more to life, than this blacked out bedroom and low vibrating energy I was experiencing. It was time I once again stop listening to the outside and go within and follow the guidance of my soul.

The question, what is it you want to do for fun was always presenting itself to me.

Fun, I want to be free. Free of all these words that are lingering in my mind. Free of the pain I'm experiencing in my body. Fun was being free of the mental imprisoned thoughts I was feeding myself and allowing others to feed me. To me this was fun, to be free!

My 30's came around the corner and once again my life shattered. Sadness came barreling down on me as my dad passed away from cancer. It was the hardest time in my life. How can God take away something that mattered the most to me, after what I have just experienced?

At this point in my life, I had extreme anger in my heart for God. I started to ignore life. I stopped listening to my soul. I didn't care about anyone or anything. I gave the universe a middle finger salute and started to live my life the way I thought was perfect.

I went back into the old me, drugs, booze and sex. If I'm going to do this, it was on my terms and nothing else mattered. Escaping reality in the buzz of the moment, a sense of liberation, celebration and freedom found me with every sip of booze slithering into my bloodstream, the latest orgasm that had temporary relief, but long term effects of unworthiness and disconnect within myself. The lack of self-love was written all over my face as my spirit was dying, my ego was coming to life. Again confusion and depression found residence within me. Thoughts of suicide started to take over my body, accompanied by how this would affect others. This didn't make sense to me, I didn't care about others, yet here I was thinking of them in the mist of wanting to take my life and just die. Repeatedly the universe had a hold of me even when I told them to leave me alone. I didn't want any part to do with these so called gifts. They were a curse, yet living life on my terms was killing me slowly.

That's when I decided to seek help from someone that understood me. I was able to connect with someone that spoke my language and I didn't have to run away from who I truly was, I can just be me.

At that time life still handed me thorns, while I was fighting with the roses.

I made up my mind welcomed God and the universe back into my life. I found fun in everything, happiness always surrounded me, but I missed it focusing on things that didn't matter.

Remembering the wisdom I received, I knew I was the director of my life.

I no longer welcomed depression, anxiety and lack in my life, I fully divorced them.

I learned that love can be painful, yet so beautiful once I allowed for the truth to be revealed.

I became friends with my ego learning the lesson before the journey was birthed, giving me time to decide if I wanted to travel down that path or not.

I learned not to make rash decisions in life that taking my time was and is an asset to further awakening in this world. If I have to make a rash decision, it's because my spirit is pushing me towards it as my ego is cheering me on.

The first thing I needed to do was, stop pointing the finger at everyone else and start pointing the finger towards me. This was the hardest thing for me, how I gave away my power and most importantly why did I give it away. What was I lacking in my life at that time that I needed to fuel it with more emptiness, thinking it was fulfilling to my soul.

I learned to accept myself for who I was, there was no more hiding behind the curtain. It was time to authentically be me even if people didn't understand me, I would connect with those that understood me. Patience is key to spiritual growth and prayers are always answered.

My mindset had to match my energy, my energy had to match the actions I was practicing on a daily basis to better my life. It's impossible to feel great mentally and not want to move to receive more of the feeling; if that's the case, there is more digging to do in one of those aspects in your life. I call this the trifecta to your abundance. Emotion, thought and feelings all need to align for greatness to truly find you. This all begins in your imagination, carried over to your words, felt within your whole body, next received within your reality.

Pay attention to the life you want to create and not the life you are living. This was the number one rule I had into getting myself out of depression. Changing my thoughts instantly rather than entertaining them got me re-focused on what mattered in my life.

Remember laughter, love and joy are always surrounding you. It's your heart's desire and the universes will to deliver you everything you want.

THINK BIG, small doesn't exist in the hands of the universe.

KNOW THAT THIS IS YOUR TIME, BELIEVE IN YOURSELF and watch it all unfold for you.

Everyone has a story, it's not about everyone it's about YOU, without taking care of you, it's impossible to take care of anyone else.

This is YOUR TIME.

You got this.

Zak Lioutas

Zak "ZöE Luna" Lioutas is a Spiritual Soul Healer/Teacher and Heavens Messenger. She is assisting many on their path in meeting their higher self and accessing their greatest potential from within. Zak enjoys teaching humans a variety of methods and techniques in changing their perception of life that will benefit in healing their heart while manifesting their desires. Zak will teach you how to access a deeper sense of yourself, stand your ground, speak your truth, harness your power and live a life full of creativity, love, joy and laughter.

You may reach Zak at www.zaklioutas.com

DYNAMO DIARIES Series - *Ask us how to be a co-author in the next book!*

DYNAMO Entrepreneur
Chief Architect of WOW:
James Erdt

James Erdt is the Visionary and Founder of DYNAMO Entrepreneur, Joyzone Inc. and Fitness STAR International, which are innovative, socially responsible organizations dedicated to guiding people of all ages in fitness, nutrition and inspiration with leading edge products, speaking events and workshops. James has proven perseverance, resourcefulness and vision required to meet the greatest of challenges.

James now shares his story of overcoming addictions, negative environments, spinal surgery and near death situations as a young man with others to support and inspire them on their own life path and evolutionary journey. He is actively involved in philanthropy and chooses to give back on a global scale. Through his practical real world guidance, James shows others how to find the passion, courage, strength and most importantly, the available resources to live out their dreams with purpose while contributing to a better world in the process. His main focus is to guide others to become their best, both personally and professionally in the NOW, so they too can support their own circle of influence and lead by example.

James will support you with valuable tips, tools and some of his best success secrets inspiring joy, abundance and healthy active living.

James Erdt is available for speaking, seminars, workshops & success coaching. For bookings, please contact him directly online at:

DYNAMOentrepreneur.com
or
JamesErdt.com

Speaker, Author & Success Coach

Thank you!

Namaste,